Summary of Contents

JUMP START MYSQL

BY TIMOTHY BORONCZYK

Jump Start MySQL

by Timothy Boronczyk

Product Manager: Simon Mackie **English Editor:** Ralph Mason

Technical Editor: Peter Nijssen **Cover Designer:** Alex Walker

Published by SitePoint Pty. Ltd.

48 Cambridge Street Collingwood
VIC Australia 3066
Web: www.sitepoint.com
Email: business@sitepoint.com

ISBN 978-0-9924612-8-7 (print)

ISBN 978-0-9941826-3-0 (ebook)
Printed and bound in the United States of America

About Timothy Boronczyk

Timothy Boronczyk is a native of Syracuse, NY, where he works as a senior developer at ShoreGroup, Inc. He's been involved with Web technologies since 1998, has a degree in Software Application Programming, and is a Zend Certified Engineer. In what little spare time he has left, Timothy enjoys hanging out with friends, speaking Esperanto, and sleeping with his feet off the end of the bed. He's easily distracted by shiny objects.

About SitePoint

SitePoint specializes in publishing fun, practical, and easy-to-understand content for web professionals. Visit http://www.sitepoint.com/ to access our blogs, books, newsletters, articles, and community forums. You'll find a stack of information on JavaScript, PHP, Ruby, mobile development, design, and more.

Table of Contents

Preface

From "big data" data sets in an enterprise data center to hand-scribbled shopping lists, data is everywhere. Corporations collect as much of it as they can and analyze it to formulate new business strategies. Scientists study data looking for answers that can save lives, improve our environment, and explain our place in the universe. Even the average person maintains a fair amount of data, from ledgers detailing one's spending habits to phone numbers in a cellphone's address book. Storing and organizing all of this this data has become so easy that we often take for granted many of the database concepts and algorithms that make these things possible.

This book is an introduction to the basic concepts of working with a **Relational Database Management System** (RDBMS)—specifically, the popular, open source RDBMS MySQL. Like other installments in SitePoint's *Jump Start* series, it aims to give you a head start in your understanding of the chosen technology. You'll learn the basics quickly, in a friendly, (hopefully) pain-free way, and have a solid foundation to continue on in your learning.

I'm very grateful to have been given the opportunity to write this book. What separates it from others in the lineup is that it discusses a technology widely used both within *and* outside the world of web development. That's not to say MySQL isn't popular with developers creating web-based applications—quite the contrary! But databases are used in many other areas as well and I've tried to capture this in my selection of topics.

What is a Database?

Although we tend to associate the word **database** with the digital world of computers, the term simply refers to any organized collection of data. A database can therefore be digital/electronic or physical. The filing cabinet full of financial records that sits in the corner of your home office is a physical database. The cookbooks on your bookshelf, with their dog-eared pages and extra recipes clipped from magazines tucked inside, can also be viewed as a physical database.

In the digital world, databases are classified by how they organize and store their data. Some common types of digital databases are:

- **Flat file databases** — these store data sequentially, often in plain text files. They are easy to create and to add data to but they also have several drawbacks. Flat file databases are slow to search, may contain redundant data, and can easily become corrupted. An example of this type of database is the text file created by a solitaire game to store users' high scores.

- **Hierarchical databases** — these organize data in parent/child relationships. They are highly organized and searching is efficient, but hierarchical databases are difficult to navigate when you're not familiar with their relationships. Maintaining data relationships over time can be difficult as well. The Windows Registry is an example of a hierarchical database.

- **Key-value/document-oriented databases** — these store free-form data indexed by a key or hash value. They typically scale across wide network topologies very well but share many of the problems with flat file databases. They often contain redundant data, do not maintain relationships, and searching them can be slow. Redis and CouchDB are popular "NoSQL" database systems that manage these types of databases.

- **Relational databases** — these organize data in rows and tables, much like a printed price list or bus schedule can be organized as a table. Relational databases can support indexing large amounts of data for quick retrieval, but the relationships between tables can become very complex.

Sitting above most modern digital databases is a **database server**, an application designed specifically for managing databases, and which is responsible for marshaling access to the underlying data. We never work directly with a database in such systems. Instead, we send requests to add, update, remove, or fetch the desired data to the server. The server performs the requested actions on our behalf and forwards the results on to us. The book you're reading right now focuses on MySQL, a database server that manages relational databases.

Since the mid 1980s, **Structured Query Language** (SQL) has been the standard language used to communicate with relational database management systems. SQL consists of statements for adding, retrieving, and managing data, creating and maintaining tables, and even managing databases. Statements can be divided into categories or "sub-languages" based on their purpose: those pertaining to data storage and retrieval make up the Data Manipulation Language (DML), those for table and database management make up the Data Definition Language (DDL), and those that grant or revoke access to the database make up the Data Control Language (DCL). It's good to know about these if they come up in conversation at your next database administrator cocktail party, but I don't make such fine distinctions here. I'll refer to DML, DDL, and DCL statements all collectively as SQL.

From Codd to MySQL, a Brief History

Early databases organized their data into tree or graph structures and accessing the data required a programmer to write code to directly traverse these structures. This was a fragile approach and it was risky to add or update data, or to change the data's organization. Edgar Codd challenged this approach in 1970 in his paper *A Relational Model of Data for Large Shared Data Banks*. He argued that a superior approach would be to organize data into tables and to treat it independently from relationship, ordering, and indexing information. This was an intriguing concept at the time and engineers at IBM's San Jose Research Laboratory began work on System R, a project to prove the validity of Codd's theories.

The System R project produced the first implementation of SQL and proved that the relational concepts championed by Codd were sound. When Larry Ellison heard about the research going into the System R prototype, he was so impressed that he incorporated Codd's ideas and the SQL language into his own database server, Oracle. Incidentally, Ellison beat IBM to market in 1979 and Oracle became the first commercially available relational database management system.

Meanwhile, computer science professors at the University of California, Berkeley, had also taken an interest in Codd's paper. The university obtained funding from the National Science Foundation and the research divisions of the United States Air Force and the United States Army and set a rotating team of students—led by Michael Stonebraker—to work on University INGRES. INGRES explored many of Codd's relational ideas, but also implemented its own query language called QUEL. As students graduated and went on to work at other software companies, commercial INGRES-inspired systems and clones appeared, most notably Sybase (later licensed to Microsoft and rebranded as Microsoft SQL Server). INGRES itself was commercialized and quickly became a market leader.

INGRES' position of dominance started to decline 1985 when public sentiment shifted in favor of SQL over QUEL. SQL was accepted as a standard by both the

American National Standards Institute and the International Organization for Standards by 1987, and the decade came to a close with Oracle and SQL on top.

In 1993, David Hughes was developing a network-monitoring application that stored data in a Postgres (a successor of INGRES) managed database. For portability, he also wanted to provide an SQL interface to the data so he wrote a QUEL-to-SQL translator which he named miniSQL. As work continued on his monitoring app, Hughes grew frustrated by Postgres' hardware requirements and decided to evolve miniSQL into his own light-weight database management system. miniSQL favored a small resource footprint over complete adherence to the SQL standards, implementing only the most important subset of the standards. Hughes distributed his system for a fraction of the cost that current commercial offerings were licensed at and miniSQL went on to become the first low-cost, SQL-based relational database system. The stage was now set for MySQL.

At that same time, Monty Widenius was developing web-based applications for the still-burgeoning Internet using UNIREG, his own home-grown database server. Widenius found that accessing UNIREG to generate dynamic pages was too resource intensive and began to look for an alternative. miniSQL piqued his interest, as it had grown very popular due to its pricing strategy—especially among shared hosting providers—but it didn't implement some of the features Widenius' applications needed. He ended up rewriting UNIREG for better performance, but also took the opportunity to reimplement its API to be compatible with miniSQL's. This would allow him to take take advantage of the many third-party utilities that had sprung up for miniSQL. Widenius renamed his server MySQL and a friend convinced him to release it publicly.

MySQL was made available under the GNU General Public License, and Widenius and his friends, David Axmark and Allan Larsson, founded MySQL AB in 1995 to shepherd the development of MySQL and provide alternative licensing and support for commercial customers. Whereas miniSQL was affordable, for most users MySQL was practially free.

Since the licensing terms for MySQL were amenable for inclusion in most Linux distributions, and because its API was compatible with miniSQL but made more features available, MySQL quickly ate most of miniSQL's market share. Today, MySQL is the second most popular SQL RDBMS (the number one spot is held by SQLite thanks in large part to its use in smartphones and embedded software).

Alternatives and the Future of MySQL

Sun Microsystems bought MySQL AB in 2008 for $1 billion, and in 2010, Oracle Corporation acquired Sun Microsystems and its assets (including MySQL) for $7.4 billion. The same company that beat IBM and INGRES in the 1980s now owned the copyrights to MySQL. And Oracle already had its own flagship database, so any fears the community had about the future of MySQL under Sun were only exacerbated by the Oracle acquisition.

But thanks to the GPL, anyone can make improvements and build upon MySQL, so long as those changes are properly licensed. This means others can make enhancements to MySQL, or even fork it, and release their own version. And forks there are!

- **Dorsal Source** — the first MySQL fork made by Proven Scaling in response to complaints over Sun's slow release process and the company handled community-submitted bug fixes and enhancements. The project is now defunct.

- **Drizzle**[1] — a fork of MySQL by Brian Aker with the goal of being a faster, pared-down version of MySQL specifically for supporting web applications. Core functionality is provided by a kernel and additional features are provided by plugins. The project isn't defunct, but development seems to have stalled.

- **Percona Server**[2] — a fork maintained by the consulting firm Percona LLC. Its goal is to be a drop-in MySQL replacement that offers improved performance and various enterprise-grade features not found in Oracle's Community edition.

- **MariaDB**[3] — a fork by Monty Widenius himself in response to the Sun and Oracle acquisitions. It aims to be a community-friendly replacement that maintains feature-parity for most use cases.

---

[1] http://www.drizzle.org/

[2] http://www.percona.com/software/percona-server

[3] https://mariadb.org/

Learn More about the Forks

To learn more about the MySQL forks, watch the talk "Different MySQL Forks for Different Folks[4]" given by Sheeri Cabral at Confoo in 2013.

The long-term outlook for the MySQL "brand" is strong despite tensions in the community. Oracle hasn't shuttered MySQL as many feared, and the quality of releases has actually improved under their stewardship. The forks provide competition, which hopefully is a good thing. Even in the most cynical sense, the past decade has seen an uptick in the use of open source in the enterprise setting so MySQL won't be going anywhere anytime soon.

Who Should Read This Book

This book is aimed at those interested in working with data and want to learn how to use MySQL. To get the most out of some parts of this book, you should have some previous programming experience, although no specific language is required.

Conventions Used

You'll notice that we've used certain typographic and layout styles throughout the book to signify different types of information. Look out for the following items:

Code Samples

Code in this book will be displayed using a fixed-width font, like so:

```
<h1>A Perfect Summer's Day</h1>
<p>It was a lovely day for a walk in the park. The birds
were singing and the kids were all back at school.</p>
```

If additional code is to be inserted into an existing example, the new code will be displayed in bold:

```
function animate() {
  new_variable = "Hello";
}
```

---

[4] https://www.youtube.com/watch?v=dcWoHusSAsE

Where existing code is required for context, rather than repeat all the code, a vertical ellipsis will be displayed:

```
function animate() {
  ⋮
  return new_variable;
}
```

Some lines of code are intended to be entered on one line, but we've had to wrap them because of page constraints. A ➥ indicates a line break that exists for formatting purposes only, and should be ignored:

```
URL.open("http://www.sitepoint.com/blogs/2015/05/28/user-style-she
➥ets-come-of-age/");
```

Tips, Notes, and Warnings

Hey, You!

Tips will give you helpful little pointers.

Ahem, Excuse Me ...

Notes are useful asides that are related—but not critical—to the topic at hand. Think of them as extra tidbits of information.

Make Sure You Always ...

... pay attention to these important points.

Watch Out!

Warnings will highlight any gotchas that are likely to trip you up along the way.

Supplementary Materials

http://www.learnable.com/books/jsmysql1/
The book's website, which contains links, updates, resources, and more.

http://community.sitepoint.com/

SitePoint's forums, for help on any tricky web problems.

books@sitepoint.com

Our email address, should you need to contact us for support, to report a problem, or for any other reason.

Want to Take Your Learning Further?

Thanks for buying this book—we appreciate your support. Do you want to continue learning? You can now gain unlimited access to courses and ALL SitePoint books at Learnable for one low price. Enroll now and start learning today! Join Learnable and you'll stay ahead of the newest technology trends: http://www.learnable.com.

Getting Started with MySQL

This chapter presents the first steps of getting started with MySQL. I'll show you how to install MySQL on both Linux and Windows systems, so be sure to follow along on the platform of your choice. Then you'll begin to get acquainted with MySQL's command-line client as we use it to connect to the database server and create our first database.

Often the first step of installing an application is to determine which version is appropriate, so it's worth noting that MySQL is available in several "flavors." From Oracle there is the freely available Community Edition and the paid commercial Standard, Enterprise, and Cluster Carrier Grade editions. The differences between Community Edition and the paid versions boil down to licensing and support contracts, some additional server plugins, and backup and monitoring utilities.

MySQL is open-source software released under the GNU General Public License so it should come as no surprise there are also alternative forks available. Two popular forks are MariaDB, a community-maintained "enhanced, drop-in replacement" for MySQL, and Percona Server, a drop-in maintained by the consulting firm Percona LLC. The differences between MySQL, MariaDB, and Percona are mostly imperceptible to the casual user.

You're free to use whichever flavor of MySQL you like, but to maintain focus and consistency I'll use Oracle's Community Edition version 5.6.23 (the current stable release at the time I'm writing this book). I'll also limit these instructions to Debian/Ubuntu, RedHat/CentOS, and Windows Server 2012. This list of operating systems covers the major platforms that MySQL is likely to run on in a production environment.

Local Development Environment

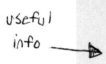

For readers looking to set up an installation for local development, I recommend creating a virtual machine using Oracle's VirtualBox[1]. You can install one of the aforementioned operating systems on the virtual machine and then install MySQL using this chapter's instructions. Not only does this give you the ability to work with a dev environment which can be configured as closely as possible to production without being tied down to a specific server or network, but also your local system remains clean from extra services and applications, whether your system is running Linux, Windows, or OS X.

Installing MySQL on Linux

Linux isn't a homogeneous platform and each distro has a preferred way to install software. In this section, I'll cover how to install MySQL on Debian/Ubuntu and Red Hat/CentOS systems using a package manager and how to compile and install MySQL from source. This will equip you with the necessary skills to handle most any Linux-based installation scenarios you may encounter.

Installing via a Package Manager

Most modern Linux systems use a package manager to make software installation a trivial task. And because it's so popular, chances are MySQL or one of its forks is available in your distro's package repositories. Debian/Ubuntu offers Oracle's MySQL Community Edition in their repos, and users can get up and running by simply typing sudo `apt-get install mysql-server`. Red Hat/CentOS repositories recently replaced MySQL with MariaDB; users can install MariaDB with su `-c 'yum install mariadb-server'`.

---

[1] https://www.virtualbox.org/

Installing software from a distro-maintained repository is fine for most users, but relying on these repos may not give you the most current release. Luckily, we don't have to give up the convenience that working with packages affords us. Oracle provides up-to-date RPM and DEB packages which can be installed using rpm and dpkg. They also maintain APT and Yum repositories and provide special packages to automatically add these repos to your system's list of known repositories.

The following steps register one of Oracle's repositories and install MySQL Community Edition from it. If your server isn't running a graphical interface and you can't use a text-based browser like Lynx, you'll need to complete the first four steps on another system and copy the file to your server.

1. Open a browser and navigate to the MySQL Repositories page at http://dev.mysql.com/downloads/repo.

2. Click the **Download** link for the **MySQL Yum Repository** or **MySQL APT Repository** depending on your platform's package manager. You'll be redirected to a page that lists various configuration packages.

3. Click the **Download** button next to the package appropriate for your system. For example, a Red Hat/CentOS 7 user should download the package **Red Hat Enterprise Linux 7 / Oracle Linux 7 (Architecture Independent), RPM Package.** An Ubuntu user using Trusty Tahr should download the package **Ubuntu Linux 14.04 (Architecture Independent), DEB.**

4. Oracle will try to trick you into signing up for an account. This isn't mandatory, so scroll down to the bottom of the page and click the link **No thanks, just start my download** to start the download.

5. Using a terminal window, navigate to the directory you downloaded (or copied) the package to and execute the appropriate command to install it:

   - Red Hat/CentOS users should run rpm -i mysql-community-release-el7-5.noarch.rpm.

   - Debian/Ubuntu users should run dpkg -i mysql-apt-config_0.2.1-1ubuntu14.04_all.deb.

6. The repository is now registered and you can install MySQL Community Edition with your package manager:

- Red Hat/CentOS users should run `su -c 'yum install mysql-community-server'`.

- Debian/Ubuntu users should run `sudo apt-get install mysql-server-5.6`.

Ubuntu users will be prompted during the installation process for a password for MySQL's root user (Debian and Red Hat/CentOS users will provide this password with a post-install command in the next step). MySQL maintains its own list of accounts separate from the user accounts on our system—that is, while the username may be the same, the MySQL root user isn't the same as the Linux root user.

Red Hat/CentOS users should run these post-install commands to set the password for MySQL's root user, register MySQL as a system service, and start a running instance (Debian/Ubuntu automatically registers and starts MySQL):

1. Set the root user's password for MySQL: `mysqladmin -u root password`.

2. Register MySQL to start when the system boots: `su -c 'chkconfig --level 2345 mysqld on'`.

3. Start the MySQL server: `su -c 'systemctl start mysql'`.

MySQL Community Edition is now installed on your system. For future reference, the following commands are used to start, stop, and check the running status of MySQL:

- **Start MySQL**

  - Ubuntu — `sudo service mysql start`

  - Debian — `sudo systemctl start mysqld`

  - Red Hat/CentOS — `su -c 'systemctl start mysql'`

- **Stop MySQL**

  - Ubuntu — `sudo service mysql stop`

  - Debian — `sudo systemctl stop mysqld`

  - Red Hat/CentOS — `su -c 'systemctl stop mysql'`

- **Query MySQL's running state**

  - Ubuntu — `service mysql status`

  - Debian — `sudo systemctl status mysqld`

  - Red Hat/CentOS — `su -c 'systemctl status mysql'`

 A Simpler Future

Different commands are used to start, stop, and monitor MySQL because Ubuntu uses Upstart and the other distros use systemd. The Ubuntu developers plan to migrate to the systemd init system starting in 15.04. By the time 16.04 LTS rolls out, the commands to perform these tasks will be the same as those on Debian.

Installing from Source

It's becoming less and less common for system administrators to compile software from source code, but doing so often gives complete control over an application's features, optimizations, and configuration settings. As you might expect, it's also the most involved installation method.

The following steps show how to download the MySQL Community Edition source code, compile it, and install it. Again, if you don't have access to a graphical interface or text-based browser on the server then you'll need to complete the first few steps on another system and copy over the download.

1. Open a browser and navigate to the MySQL Community Downloads page at http://dev.mysql.com/downloads.

2. Click the **MySQL Community Server** link to be taken to the Download MySQL Community Server page. The various platform options are filtered by the drop-down labeled **Select Platform**.

3. Set the drop-down to **Source Code**, scroll down to the **Generic Linux (Architecture Independent), Compressed TAR Archive** entry, and click its **Download** button.

4. An Oracle account isn't mandatory for continuing with the download. Scroll to the bottom of the page and click the link **No thanks, just start my download** to begin the download.

5. Using a terminal window, create a new user account dedicated solely to running the MySQL server:

```
sudo groupadd mysql
sudo useradd -r -g mysql mysql
```

6. Navigate to the directory you downloaded the source archive to. Extract the archive and change into the code's directory:

```
cd /tmp
gzip -cd mysql-5.6.23.tar.gz | tar xvf -
cd mysql-5.6.23
```

7. Generate the build scripts by running cmake. I don't specify any options below, but a full list of configuration options can be found in the online documentation[2].

```
cmake .
```

8. Run make to compile MySQL, and then with elevated privileges run make install to copy the resulting binaries, utilities, libraries, and documentation files to their new home on your system:

```
make
sudo make install
```

9. Make sure the installed files are assigned the correct ownership and access permissions:

```
sudo chown -R mysql /usr/local/mysql
sudo chgrp -R mysql /usr/local/mysql
```

10. MySQL's data directory and system tables need to be initialized by the mysql_install_db script found in the installation's scripts directory. The script

---

[2] http://dev.mysql.com/doc/refman/5.6/en/source-configuration-options.html

uses paths relative to the installation directory, so invoke it from the installation directory rather than the `scripts` directory or somewhere else:

```
cd /usr/local/mysql
sudo scripts/mysql_install_db --user=mysql
```

11. Start MySQL and set its root user's password:

```
sudo mysqld_safe &
mysqladmin -u root password
```

The installation of MySQL itself is complete, but there's still some additional system configuration tasks you should consider. I recommend adding the installation's `bin` directory to the PATH environment variable so you can run MySQL's utilities without providing a full path each time. Assuming you use Bash, add the following lines to `/etc/profile`:

```
PATH=/usr/local/mysql/bin:$PATH
export PATH
```

 Working with PATH

Setting the value of PATH in `/etc/profile` makes the utilities conveniently accessible for all system users. If you only want your own account to have this ability then add the lines to your `~/.bash_profile` or `~/.bashrc` file instead.

It's also likely you'll want MySQL to start automatically when the system boots. These steps assume your system uses a SysV-style init process.

1. Place a copy of the `mysql.server` script found in the source code's `support-files` directory in your system's `init.d` directory and make the script executable:

```
sudo cp /tmp/mysql-5.6.23/support-files/mysql.server \
/etc/init.d/mysql
sudo chmod 755 /etc/init.d/mysql
```

2. Create symbolic links that point to the script from the desired runlevels:

```
ln -s /etc/init.d/mysql /etc/rc3.d/S99mysql
ln -s /etc/init.d/mysql /etc/rc0.d/K01mysql
```

You can now run the command `sudo /etc/init.d/mysql start` to start MySQL and run `sudo /etc/init.d/mysql stop` to stop it.

Installing MySQL on Windows

Windows is a relatively homogeneous platform compared to Linux even though several versions of the OS are actively maintained at any given time by Microsoft. The instructions here target Server 2012, but may be more or less applicable to a desktop OS like Windows 8.

1. Open a browser and navigate to the MySQL Community Downloads page at http://dev.mysql.com/downloads.

2. Click the link for **MySQL Community Server** to be taken to the Download MySQL Community Server page. The various platform options here are filtered by the drop-down labeled **Select Platform**.

3. Set the drop-down to **Microsoft Windows** and click the **Download** button next to the appropriate Windows MSI Installer for your architecture, most likely 64-bit.

4. Scroll to the bottom of the page and click the link **No thanks, just start my download** to begin the download.

5. Navigate to the folder you downloaded the MSI file to and double-click the file to launch the installation wizard.

6. Advance through the wizard's welcome screen by pressing the **Next** button.

7. At the **License Agreement** screen, click the checkbox to accept the terms of the agreement, and press **Next**.

8. At the **Choose Setup Type** screen, choose **Typical**, then press the **Install** button to begin the installation. You may be prompted by User Account Control to proceed depending on the security policies in effect.

9. Press the **Finish** button once the wizard is finished.

Now follow these post-install configuration steps to add the installation's `bin` directory to the system `PATH` variable and register MySQL as a service.

1. Open the **System Properties** window.

   a. Press the key combination **WIN-C** to bring up the Edge UI.

   b. Click the **Search** charm, search for Control Panel, and click on the **Control Panel** icon when it appears in the results.

   c. If Control Panel is in **Category** view, click the **System and Security** entry and then **System** to launch the System panel item. If Control Panel is in **Icon** view, click the **System** icon.

2. Click the **Advanced systems settings** link to open the **System Properties** window.

3. Select the **Advanced** tab if it's not already selected and then press the **Environment Variables** button to open the **Environment Variables** window.

4. Select the **Path** entry in the **System variables** section and press the **Edit** button.

5. Add the `bin` directory's path (`C:\Program Files\MySQL\MySQL Server 5.6\bin`) to the end of the existing value, separating the entry from the previous entries with a semicolon.

6. Open Command Prompt with administrator privileges. Depending on the security policies in effect, you may be prompted by User Account Control to continue.

   a. Press the key combination **WIN-C** to bring up the Edge UI.

   b. Click the **Search** charm and search for Command Prompt.

   c. Right-click the **Command Prompt** icon when it appears in the results and select **Run as administrator**.

7. Run `mysqld.exe --install` at the prompt. The command should report back the service was successfully installed.

You're now able to invoke the utilities when using Command Prompt without providing their full path because MySQL's `bin` directory appears in the list that Windows searches for executables. And since MySQL is registered as a service, it will start automatically when the system boots and can be controlled from Windows Service Manager. Alternatively, the following commands may be executed in Command Prompt with administrator privileges to start and stop the MySQL server as well.

- **Start MySQL** — `net start mysql`

- **Stop MySQL** — `net stop mysql`

Communicating with the Server

A MySQL server sits idle, waiting to receive queries. When it receives one, the server performs the requested action on our behalf and responds back with the result. There are several ways we can communicate with MySQL, for example programmatically from an application we wrote or interactively using a dedicated client program. We'll use the command-line client that's included in the MySQL installation to connect and communicate with the running server throughout most of this book, and in Chapter 5 we'll discuss sending SQL statements programmatically.

Open a terminal window or Command Prompt and run `mysql -u root -p`. The `-u` option specifies the username of the MySQL account used for the connection and `-p` will prompt for the account's password. When prompted, enter the root account's password you set earlier.

 Options Galore

`-u` and `-p` are just two of many options accepted by the client. Here's a list of some other options you may find yourself using frequently (you can call the client with the option `-?` for a complete listing):

- `-A` — don't re-initialize the auto-complete lookup

- `-B` — run in batch mode

- `-e` *statement* — execute the given SQL statement

- `-h` *hostname* — specify a hostname to a remote database server

- `-N` — suppress column names from the result output

- `-p` — prompt for the account's password to connect

- -u *username* — specify the username of an account to connect

- -? — list all of the available options

The client displays the mysql> prompt once you've successfully connected to MySQL. It's at this prompt we'll submit our SQL statements. The client displays the server's response, timing information for how long it took to execute the request, and whether any errors or warnings were encountered.

The MySQL server is capable of managing more than one database at a time. To ask what databases it's managing, enter SHOW DATABASES; at the prompt. The response will show a list of all the databases MySQL is managing. If you're connected to a newly installed instance then you'll only see the three databases that are used by MySQL itself: information_schema, mysql, and performance_schema. You may also see a test database which is created by mysql_install_db for use as a sandbox.

The CREATE DATABASE statement creates a new database. To create a database named "jumpstart", send the statement CREATE DATABASE jumpstart; at the prompt. Then send SHOW DATABASES; again, and you'll see the new database added to the list.

To let the client know we want to work with a specific database, we use the USE command. Enter USE jumpstart; at the prompt, and all subsequent statements we send will be executed against the jumpstart database. It's possible to specify a target database when connecting with the command-line client, for example mysql -u root -p jumpstart.

The SHOW TABLES statement instructs MySQL to return a list of tables in the currently active database. Of course, we haven't added any tables to the jumpstart database yet so sending SHOW TABLES; will be met with the response "Empty set." There's a fair bit of planning involved to create a table properly, and we've covered a lot already, so I'll save that for the next chapter.

To quit the client, either type exit or use the key combination **CTRL-D**.

MySQL Accounts and Security

The final thing I feel the need to cover in this chapter is MySQL user accounts. Even though MySQL's root user isn't the same as the system's root account, it's still not intended to be used on a regular basis. The MySQL root user should only be used for administrative tasks such as creating new user accounts, setting permissions, and flushing access caches. Less privileged accounts should be used on a day-to-day basis.

To create a new user account, connect to the MySQL server with the command-line client using the root account and send the following CREATE USER statement:

```
CREATE USER 'jump'@'localhost' IDENTIFIED BY 'secret';
```

The statement creates a new account with the username "jump" and password "secret" that will permit the user to authenticate from the same system MySQL is running on. Different hostnames and IP addresses can be used in place of localhost to allow connections from different systems and networks. However, bear in mind that MySQL considers each username/hostname pair to be a separate account. That is, jump@localhost and jump@192.168.1.100 are treated as separate accounts, each with their own set of privileges.

Wildcards

The _ and % characters are wildcards that can be used in the hostname part to provide partial matches, for example "192.168.1.10_" or "%.example.com". _ matches a single character and % matches any number of characters. Thus, the following can be used to create an account capable of authenticating from any system—a convenient but potentially very insecure practice:

```
CREATE USER 'jump'@'%' IDENTIFIED BY 'secret';
```

Whether MySQL permits a user to perform an activity depends on what privileges are associated with the account. New accounts are created without any privileges so we must explicitly grant any that the account will need. The "jump" user will require several privileges as you use it to follow along throughout the rest of this book. For now, let's grant a basic set of privileges to start with (you can grant additional privileges as they become necessary). Enter the following statement:

```
GRANT CREATE, DROP, ALTER, INSERT, UPDATE, SELECT, DELETE,
INDEX ON jumpstart.* TO 'jump'@'localhost';
```

The syntax of MySQL's GRANT statement is flexible enough that we can narrow the scope of a privilege down to specific columns of a table, or to certain tables in a database. Here, we've simply instructed MySQL to allow these permissions for all tables (denoted by the *) in our jumpstart database. The privileges granted are:

- CREATE — allows the user to create databases and tables

- DROP — allows the user to delete entire tables and databases

- ALTER — allows the user to change the definition of an existing table

- INSERT — allows the user to add records to a table

- UPDATE — allows the user to update existing records in a table

- SELECT — allows the user to retrieve existing records from a table

- DELETE — allows the user to delete existing records from a table

- INDEX — allows the user to create or delete indexes

A full list of privileges and what they allow an account to do can be found in the documentation[3]. In the future, if it's determined an account needs extra privileges then they can be granted by issuing another GRANT statement. Privileges that are no longer needed can be revoked with a REVOKE statement, the syntax of which is identical to that of GRANT:

```
REVOKE CREATE, DROP, ALTER, INDEX ON jumpstart.* TO
'jump'@'localhost';
```

Whenever a user-related or privilege-related change is made, we need to send a FLUSH PRIVILEGES statement to instruct MySQL to reload the cache of account information it maintains so the updates can take effect. Otherwise, the changes will go unnoticed until MySQL is restarted:

---

[3] http://dev.mysql.com/doc/refman/5.6/en/privileges-provided.html

```
FLUSH PRIVILEGES;
```

Exit the command-line client after you send the FLUSH PRIVILEGES statement and reconnect using the new "jump" account. If you've entered the statements correctly, and provided the correct password when prompted, you'll be greeted with the mysql> prompt.

Conclusion

We've definitely covered a lot of ground in this chapter. You've learned how to install MySQL on various platforms, how to connect to a MySQL server using the command-line client, how to create a new database, and even a bit about basic MySQL user management.

Although you may be anxious to dive into the next chapter, I suggest you skim through the online MySQL manual first—specifically to see what it has to say on the topics we've covered so far. Review the details of the CREATE USER and GRANT statements. Learn how to change an account's password and how to delete an account that's no longer needed. Think about what privileges you'd assign to an account that needs to store and retrieve data as part of some back-end process for a website.

In Chapter 2, we'll get into the specifics of storing data in a database. I'll show you how to create a table and insert new rows into it. We'll also discuss what types of data can be stored in a table, what a storage engines is, and how our choice of engine affects the way MySQL manages our data.

Storing Data

Data stored in a relational database is organized into **tables**. A database table organizes data in a grid-like fashion, where each entry forms a **row** and each **column** identifies a specific value in the entry. To illustrate this, here's a table showing the number of medals won by each of the top five medal-winning countries that participated in the 2014 Winter Olympic Games. Each row lists the country's name, how many gold medals, silver medals, and bronze medals were won, and the total number of medals won.

Country	Gold	Silver	Bronze	Total
Russia	13	11	9	33
United States	9	7	12	28
Norway	11	5	10	26
Canada	10	10	5	25
Netherlands	8	7	9	24

A table like the one above is "physical" in that we can see it printed in a book or drawn on a whiteboard. It's limited only by the amount of physical space available.

On the other hand, a database table is an intangible structure stored somewhere on a hard drive or in computer memory. We can only imagine it or make drawings to represent it. A database table is interpreted by a computer process (such as MySQL), and the limitations of the interpreting process impose restrictions on the table. The number of columns, the number of rows, and even what the individual values in a row can be, all depend upon what the computer system and database server can handle. But despite these limitations, a database table is actually very flexible. We can define relationships between tables, combine multiple tables together, sort rows and view specific entries, remove rows, and easily perform various calculations on the data.

In this chapter, we'll look at the CREATE TABLE statement—which defines new database tables—and discuss some important details surrounding table creation: MySQL's supported data types, naming restrictions, and storage engines. We'll also see how to add rows to a table with the INSERT statement, and finish by discussing transactions.

Creating Tables

Tables are created using the CREATE TABLE statement. In its simplest form, the statement provides the name of the table we we want to create and a list of column names and their data types. Not surprisingly, a CREATE TABLE statement can be very very complex depending on the requirements driving the design of the table. We can specify one or more attributes as part of a column's definition; such attributes can limit the range of values the column can store or specify a default value when one isn't provided by the user. Defining any logical relationships that exist between the table and another, and which storage engine MySQL should use to manage the table, is also common. You can see how detailed the statement can be if you look at the syntax and options for CREATE TABLE in the MySQL documentation[1].

Let's take a look at a pair of relatively simple CREATE TABLE statements. (I'll highlight some common points that add complexity, but I won't get too crazy, I promise.) With the jumpstart database created in Chapter 1 as your active database, issue the statements below. MySQL should respond "Query OK" after each one.

---

[1] http://dev.mysql.com/doc/refman/5.6/en/create-table.html

```
CREATE TABLE employee (
    employee_id INTEGER UNSIGNED NOT NULL AUTO_INCREMENT,
    last_name VARCHAR(30) NOT NULL,
    first_name VARCHAR(30) NOT NULL,
    email VARCHAR(100) NOT NULL,
    hire_date DATE NOT NULL,
    notes MEDIUMTEXT,

    PRIMARY KEY (employee_id),
    INDEX (last_name),
    UNIQUE (email)
)
ENGINE=InnoDB;

CREATE TABLE address (
    employee_id INTEGER UNSIGNED NOT NULL,
    address VARCHAR(50) NOT NULL,
    city VARCHAR(30) NOT NULL,
    state CHAR(2) NOT NULL,
    postcode CHAR(5) NOT NULL,

    FOREIGN KEY (employee_id)
        REFERENCES employee (employee_id)
)
ENGINE=InnoDB;
```

The first statement creates a table named employee, designed to store basic information about a company's employees—their name, email address, date of hire, and
perhaps any notes the Human Resources director might provide. The formatting is
just to keep things readable for ourselves; it makes no difference to MySQL whether
we write a statement entirely on one line or across several lines with indentation.
The spacing in a statement is also generally irrelevant.

 Local Bias

The address table has a North American bias. An address in the United States
or Mexico fits perfectly, and a Canadian address can store the two-letter province
or territory abbreviation in the state column. But an address in the Netherlands,
for example, needs space for a 6-character postal code. Feel free to adapt the
definition to your own locale.

Names chosen for a table and its columns can be anything we like so long as they adhere to the following restrictions:

- The name uses basic Latin letters (A–Z, both uppercase and lowercase), the dollar sign ($), underscore (_), or Unicode characters U+0080–U+FFFF.

- The null character 0x00, Unicode characters U+10000 and higher, and characters that are prohibited in file names like slash (/), backslash (\), and period are not allowed in a name.

- The name must be quoted if it contains characters outside of the above. MySQL uses backticks by default for this (`…`) although it can be configured to use single quotes ('…') as well. I recommend sticking with the default.

- The name must be quoted if it's a MySQL reserved keyword. A list of reserved words can be found in the online documentation[2].

The employee_id column is designated as the table's **primary key**. A primary key is a column in which all of the values are distinct and can be used to uniquely identify each and every row in the table. In more complex table definitions, we may define a primary key from multiple columns together, but using a single INTEGER type column is the most common practice. Only one primary key can be defined per table (hence the name *primary* key).

The employee_id column also has the AUTO_INCREMENT attribute. Whenever we add a row that doesn't provide a value for this column, MySQL will automatically use the next highest sequential integer as its value. Suppose we have a number of rows in the employee table and the largest employee_id value among them is 42. If we add a new row without an employee_id value, MySQL will use 43 for the missing value. If we then add another row without the value, MySQL will use 44, and so on. Only one column in the table can be designated an auto-increment column, and the column must also be a primary key.

Behind the scenes, MySQL maintains various data structures to track data and relationships. The INDEX defined on last_name lets MySQL know that we might use its value in our selection criteria later when we retrieve rows—for example, if we wanted to search for employees named Smith or Jones. MySQL will create and

---

[2] http://dev.mysql.com/doc/refman/5.6/en/reserved-words.html

manage a special index structure with the values in the column to make its search more efficient. Don't go overboard adding indexes though. It takes time for MySQL to maintain them so row retrieval may be faster, but adding/updating rows will be slower.

The term **constraint** describes a special condition imposed on a column or table that must be adhered to at all times. Most of the column definitions have NOT NULL, a constraint that prohibits storing NULL values in the column. NULL is a special value that represents the absence of a value. Essentially, NOT NULL means the column *must* hold a value. MySQL treats NULL differently from an empty value, such as an empty text string.

The UNIQUE constraint defined on the email column ensures all of the email addresses stored in the table are different. UNIQUE and PRIMARY KEY are similar, but there are important differences between them. Because the values in a primary key column must be able to unambiguously identify each row, its uniqueness is inherent. We don't explicitly specify UNIQUE with PRIMARY KEY. And while only one primary key can be defined per table, we can provide any number of UNIQUE constraints. A UNIQUE column may also contain NULL values, something PRIMARY KEY doesn't allow.

The FOREIGN KEY constraint in the address table's CREATE TABLE statement references the employee table, thus defining a relationship between the two tables. This relationship means that a row in the address table is logically related to whatever row in the employee table that has the same value in its employee_id column. Take, for instance, a row in the address table with an employee_id value of 42. That row may be associated with the row in the employee table whose employee_id value is also 42. In other words, an address with employee_id 42 is linked to employee 42's employee record. A FOREIGN KEY column doesn't need to have the same name as its partner column in the other table, but the two must share the same data type and NULL constraint.

We can issue DESCRIBE or SHOW CREATE TABLE statements to verify a table was created or view the definition of an existing table. The DESCRIBE statement returns the list of the table's column names and their data types, and SHOW CREATE TABLE returns a statement that can be used later to re-create the table.

```
DESCRIBE employee;

SHOW CREATE TABLE employee;
```

 Pick a Convention

A convention I've adopted is to type MySQL keywords in uppercase and my own identifiers in lowercase. MySQL doesn't treat keywords and column names in a case-sensitive manner, but table names might be case-sensitive depending on the file system storing your tables' files. It's best to pick a convention—whatever it may be—and stick with it.

So far, we've discussed the column attributes and table constraints that appear in the example, but we haven't discussed the data types. The next part of this chapter may be a little dry, but it covers some important information. Each type requires a different amount of storage on disk and in memory so we always want to specify the minimum viable type for a column. The amount of wasted space from assigning a data type that's larger than necessary might be negligible at first because there's only a handful of rows, but it can add up quickly as more and more data is added to the table.

Data Types and Storage Requirements

MySQL supports many different data types, most of which we'll discuss in the following paragraphs. The term **data type** refers to the classification of data based on its possible values, the set of operations we can perform on it, and its storage requirements. Values of the INTEGER type can only consist of integers like 0, 42, and 1337. This is different from the DECIMAL type which consists of decimal numbers like 1.61, 3.14, and 100.0. We can perform operations like addition, subtraction, multiplication, and division on INTEGER and DECIMAL values, but these cannot be performed on text-based types like CHAR and TEXT.

Numeric Types

MySQL offers the INTEGER (also abbreviated as INT), TINYINT, SMALLINT, MEDIUMINT, and BIGINT data types for storing integer data. These types differ in the number of bytes they occupy to represent a value. This in turn limits the range of integers each type can hold. For example, TINYINT uses 1 byte, so its range is -128 to 127—the range of numbers than can be expressed in binary with 8 bits. INTEGER uses 4 bytes, so its range is larger: -2,147,483,648 to 2,147,483,647.

We can also specify the UNSIGNED attribute with integer-based types. The type consumes the same amount of space but negative values are disallowed in exchange for raising the upper bound. For example, the range of TINYINT UNSIGNED becomes 0 to 255. Both TINYINT and TINYINT UNSIGNED represent a range of 256 integers, but their starting points are -128 and 0 respectively.

The following table shows the storage requirements and range for each of MySQL's integer types, both signed and unsigned:

Data Type	Storage Used (Bytes)	Min. Signed	Max. Signed	Max. Unsigned
TINYINT	1	-128	127	255
SMALLINT	2	-32,768	32,767	65,535
MEDIUMINT	3	-8,388,608	8,388,607	6,777,215
INTEGER	4	-2,147,483,648	2,147,483,647	4,294,967,295
BIGINT	8	-9,223,372,036,854,775,808	9,223,372,036,854,775, 807	18,446,744,073,709,551,615

DECIMAL, FLOAT, and DOUBLE are types that support real numbers. We also must provide the precision (the number of total digits) and scale (the number of digits that follow the decimal point) when we use one of these types. DECIMAL(5,2) has a range of -999.99 to 999.99—that is, five digits in total with two of them following the decimal point. We can specify UNSIGNED for these types as well, but doing so only disallows negative values. This is because the upper limit is defined by the precision and scale we provide.

The DECIMAL type is a fixed-point data type which means it preserves the exact precision of its value in calculations. This is useful for representing values like monetary amounts. The maximum precision we can specify for DECIMAL is 65, and the maximum scale is 30. On the other hand, FLOAT and DOUBLE are both floating-point types. Calculations with these types are approximate because some rounding may occur due to how the values are represented internally in the computer. The difference between FLOAT and DOUBLE is the amount of space they occupy, which in turn affects their accuracy. FLOAT is 4-byte single-precision which is generally accurate up to 7 decimal places. DOUBLE is 8-byte double-precision which is generally accurate up to 15 decimal places.

The BIT data type stores a bit-sequence. This is useful for storing bit-field values like flags and bit masks. BIT has a capacity of 1 to 64 bits. BIT(1) can only hold 0 or 1; BIT(2) can hold the binary values 00, 01, 10, and 11; BIT(3) can hold the binary values 000, 001, 010, 011, 100, 101, 110, and 111, and so on. MySQL uses the notation b'value' to specify the value as string of binary digits, like b'101010'.

String Types

MySQL devotes several data types to storing textual data: CHAR, VARCHAR, BINARY, VARBINARY, TEXT, TINYTEXT, MEDIUMTEXT, LONGTEXT, BLOB, TINYBLOB, MEDIUMBLOB, and LONGBLOB. The sized types like TINYTEXT and MEDIUMTEXT behave exactly like TEXT although each is constrained by a different maximum amount of text it can hold. The same is true for BLOB and its sized counterparts, TINYBLOB, MEDIUMBLOB, and LONGBLOB.

We must provide a length when we specify a CHAR or VARCHAR type. CHAR(255), for instance, stores text strings 255 characters long, and VARCHAR(255) stores strings up to 255 characters in length. Notice that I said "255 characters" and "*up to* 255 characters." CHAR is intended to store fixed-length strings, values that will always have the same number of characters across all rows in the table. The amount of space remains constant. VARCHAR stores variable-length strings, values that can have different lengths across the rows. The amount of space each value occupies is determined by the length of the string.

useful Info I'll highlight the difference between CHAR and VARCHAR using the string "Hello World". The string is 11 characters long, and it will occupy 11 bytes (plus an extra byte or two that MySQL needs to add for its own bookkeeping) if we store it in a VARCHAR(255) column. But with CHAR(255), the storage space is constant across all rows in the table. MySQL pads the string with 244 spaces. The padding is removed when we retrieve the string and the original 11-character "Hello World" string is returned, but all CHAR(255) strings occupy 255 bytes when they're stored.

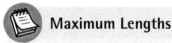 **Maximum Lengths**

> CHAR and VARCHAR have different maximum lengths. CHAR is allowed up to 255 characters and VARCHAR is allowed up to 65,535 characters. You probably won't want to use VARCHAR(65535) though. MySQL limits the size of a row to 25,535 bytes. Almost all of the row's columns contribute to the size (TEXT and BLOB are excluded), so you wouldn't have space left for the other columns. You find detailed information about the limits on row and column sizes in the online documentation[3].

BINARY and VARBINARY behave similarly to CHAR and VARCHAR except they're used for binary strings. MySQL treats binary strings as a series of bytes, not characters, and doesn't take collation or character set into consideration when working with them. No special semantics are applied; any sorting or comparison operations performed are based on the ordinal value of each byte. MySQL uses the NULL byte 0x00 to pad/strip BINARY values.

TEXT and BLOB are variable-length data types for storing larger amounts of text. Neither performs padding/stripping, which makes them ideal for preserving the exact nature of the data. TEXT values are treated as character strings and BLOB values are treated as binary strings. The TEXT and BLOB columns (and their sized variants) are also excluded when MySQL calculates the length of a row, so consider using one of them when you need to store more than 65,535 bytes of data.

The non-binary string types CHAR, VARCHAR, and TEXT can be given the CHARACTER SET attribute to specify the data's encoding. A **character set** determines how the underlying bits and bytes are interpreted as human-readable characters. Common sets include ASCII (ascii), ISO 8859-1 (latin1), and UTF-8 (utf8). The default character set when none is specified is latin1.

```
CREATE TABLE charset_example (
    id INTEGER UNSIGNED NOT NULL AUTO_INCREMENT,
    ascii_string VARCHAR(255) CHARACTER SET ascii NOT NULL,
    latin1_string VARCHAR(255) CHARACTER SET latin1 NOT NULL,
    utf8_string VARCHAR(255) CHARACTER SET utf8 NOT NULL,
```

---

[3] https://dev.mysql.com/doc/refman/5.6/en/column-count-limit.html

```
    PRIMARY KEY (id)
);
```

The ENUM and SET data types restrict a value to those allowed by a defined list. A column defined as ENUM('Alpha', 'Beta', 'Gamma') can only contain one of the strings listed in the definition, either "Alpha", "Beta", or "Gamma". SET holds strings with one or more comma-separated values from its list. SET('Alpha', 'Beta', 'Gamma') can hold values like "Alpha", "Alpha,Beta,Gamma", "Beta,Gamma", and so on.

Use ENUM with Caution

I have nothing against ENUM when it's use suits my data, but this seemingly inno-cent data type is not without controversy. Chris Komlenic's blog post "8 Reasons Why MySQL's ENUM Data Type Is Evil"[4] is a good read on the subject.

The following table shows the storage requirements and the maximum length allowed for MySQL's string types:

Data Type	Storage Used (Bytes)	Maximum
CHAR(m)	m × maximum-size character in the character set	255 chars
VARCHAR (m)	up to 2 bytes + m × maximum-size character in the character set	65,535 chars
TEXT	size of string in bytes + 2	65,535 chars
TINYTEXT	size of string in bytes + 1	255 chars
MEDIUMTEXT	size of string in bytes + 3	16,777,215 chars
LONGTEXT	size of string in bytes + 4	4,294,967,295 chars
BINARY(m)	m	255 bytes
VARBINARY(m)	up to 2 bytes + m	65,535 bytes

---

[4] http://komlenic.com/244

Data Type	Storage Used (Bytes)	Maximum
BLOB	size of string in bytes + 2	65,535 bytes
TINYBLOB	size of string in bytes + 1	255 bytes
MEDIUMBLOB	size of string in bytes + 3	16,777,215 bytes
LONGBLOB	size of string in bytes + 4	4,294,967,295 bytes
ENUM	up to 2 bytes	65,535 values
SET	up to 8 bytes	64 members

Temporal Types

The data types DATETIME, TIMESTAMP, DATE, TIME, and YEAR are for working with date and time values. Both DATETIME and TIMESTAMP hold values containing date and time parts using the format 'YYYY-MM-DD HH:mm:ss' (YYYY is a four-digit year, MM is a two-digit month, DD a two-digit day, HH a two-digit hour, mm two-digit minutes, and ss two-digit seconds). For example, '2015-03-15 13:15:00' is 1:15 p.m. on the third of March, 2015. The DATE, TIME, and YEAR types all store their single respective part values. Besides 'HH:mm:ss' to represent a time of day—such as 13:15:00—TIME values may also be given like 'HHH:mm:ss' to represent an elapsed amount of time—such as 293:23:10, meaning 293 hours, 23 minutes, and 10 seconds.

MySQL can automatically initialize and update DATETIME and TIMESTAMP values with the current date and time whenever a row is added or updated. If the INSERT statement adds a new row to the table but doesn't have a value for the TIMESTAMP column, MySQL will use the current date and time as the value. MySQL also updates a TIMESTAMP column's value when any of the values in its row are updated. While this behavior is automatic for TIMESTAMP, we can also apply it to DATETIME columns by specifying the attributes DEFAULT CURRENT_TIMESTAMP and ON UPDATE CURRENT_TIMESTAMP in the column definition.

Variations in Temporal Types

There are a few subtleties to the behavior of temporal data types across different releases of MySQL, especially with **TIMESTAMP** and **YEAR**. Review the documentation on timestamp initialization[5] and two-digit years[6].

The following table shows the range and storage requirements for each of MySQL's temporal types:

Data Type	Storage Used (Bytes)	Minimum	Maximum
DATETIME	8	1000-01-01 00:00:00	9999-12-31 23:59:59
TIMESTAMP	4	1970-01-01 00:00:01 UTC	2038-01-19 03:14:07 UTC
DATE	3	1000-01-01	9999-12-31
TIME	3	-838:59:59	838:59:59
YEAR	1	1901	2155

Spacial Data Types

The Open Geospatial Consortium has published a large number of standards focused on the representation of geographic information in various formats. MySQL offers a few types based on the consortium's work for storing such data: POINT, LINESTRING, POLYGON, GEOMETRY, MULTIPOINT, MULTISTRING, MULTIPOLYGON, and GEOMETRYCOLLECTION.

The POINT, LINESTRING, and POLYGON types each support the geometric values suggested by their names. A POINT holds the coordinates of a single point, like Point(10, 20), and a LINESTRING holds point pairs that define a line, like LineString(Point(10, 20), Point(30, 20)). The GEOMETRY type is a super-type that can hold both POINT and LINESTRING values. The MULTI* and GEOMETRYCOLLECTION types support multiple members of the same values that their singular counterparts

---

[5] http://dev.mysql.com/doc/refman/5.6/en/timestamp-initialization.html
[6] http://dev.mysql.com/doc/refman/5.6/en/two-digit-years.html

do. For example, a `MULTIPOINT` column can hold several points like `Multi-Point(Point(10, 20), Point(20, 20), Point(30, 20))`.

Working with spacial data can be a discipline in itself, so we won't discuss it further. The following resources are a good starting point (no pun intended) if you're interested in learning more about the facilities MySQL has for working with spacial data:

- MySQL Manual: Extensions for Spatial Data[7]

- MySQL GIS Forum[8]

- Open Geospatial Consortium[9]

Storage Engines

The term **storage engine** refers to the underlying logic and programming code responsible for managing our tables and data. An engine principally abstracts away the specific details of how data might be organized on the disk or in memory and allows us to think of it simply in terms of tables and rows. But different engines also have different abilities and restrictions. MySQL implements a pluggable architecture that gives us the ability to select different storage engines as we see fit, and different tables can be managed by different engines even in the same database.

You can issue a `SHOW ENGINES` statement to see a list of storage engines available to your MySQL server.

```
SHOW ENGINES;
```

InnoDB has been MySQL's default storage engine since MySQL 5.5 and a `CREATE STATEMENT` that doesn't include the `ENGINE` clause will result in a table managed by this engine. InnoDB is **ACID-compliant,** which means every transaction—one or more statements sent to the server that must be treated as a single whole—must observe the following four constraints:

---

[7] http://dev.mysql.com/doc/refman/5.6/en/spatial-extensions.html
[8] http://forums.mysql.com/list.php?23
[9] http://www.opengeospatial.org

- **Atomicity** — Each transaction is committed in its entirety or not at all. If part of a transaction fails—perhaps one statement fails in the middle of the batch—then the data must be returned to the state it was in before the start of the transaction.

- **Consistency** — All changes made by a transaction must leave the data in a valid state as defined by any constraints and other rules. This means that no foreign key constraints can be violated, there can be no disallowed values (such as a NULL in a NOT NULL column), and so on.

- **Isolation** — All transactions must be isolated from one another. Two transactions that occur at the same time must not affect or be affected by each other.

- **Durability** — Once a transaction's changes are committed, they are final and can't be rolled back.

The InnoDB engine also employs row-level locking. Whenever an engine's process writes a row to a table, it needs to make sure another process isn't attempting to write to the same location at the same time. To prevent this, the writing process establishes a lock, writes the data, and then releases the lock. The other process must wait until the lock is free before it can establish its own lock. Several processes can add and update data concurrently in the same table, just not the same row in the table.

With its ACID compliance and row-level locking strategy, InnoDB is a good choice when you need a reliable, general-purpose storage engine.

MyISAM was the default storage engine prior to MySQL 5.5. It's based on the original UNIREG's rewritten ISAM engine, and as such its focus is speed and maintaining a small resource footprint. MyISAM trades ACID compliance and features like foreign-key enforcement for faster performance. Because MyISAM doesn't have the overhead that comes with ensuring ACID behavior, the engine is a good choice for mostly read-only data, and when you're forced to run MySQL on low-end hardware.

MyISAM implements a table-level locking strategy. The lock is held against the entire table and no two processes can add or update data in the same table at the same time. This means MyISAM has a lower level of concurrency than InnoDB.

In addition to InnoDB and MyISAM, Oracle MySQL also other storage engines:

- Archive — The Archive engine is useful if you need to save a large amount of data but will rarely access it. New rows are compressed and appended to the table's existing data. Rows are uncompressed on-demand when we retrieve them. The compression helps the data to consume less disk space, but it also means MySQL can't rely on indexes to efficiently search the data; MySQL has to scan through the entire table's contents to find matching rows. The compress/append strategy also means statements like DELETE, UPDATE, and REPLACE aren't supported.

- Blackhole — The Blackhole engine behaves like a /dev/null device. It accepts any data we send and then immediately discards it. To borrow from the tagline of a particular brand of insect trap, "data checks in, but it doesn't check out". The engine is useful for testing and development scenarios and for setting up a repeater system in a replicated environment.

- CSV — The CSV engine stores comma-separated data in text files. These files are easily handled by spreadsheet applications, like Microsoft Excel or OpenOffice Calc, which makes it useful to transfer a table's data to or from a spreadsheet, or export the data to some automated process. However, many limitations are imposed to ensure the integrity of the CSV file. It doesn't support primary and foreign keys, various constraints, or columns that allow NULL values.

- Federated — The Federated engine is useful when you need to work with data from a remote MySQL table as if it were local. No data is stored locally for a Federated-managed table. Instead, all rows are read from and written to the remote database. Keep in mind that performance is slower when working with remote data as opposed to local data, and indexes are not supported, because access to the actual data is managed by the remote server.

- Merge — MyISAM tables are limited in size by restrictions put in place by the operating system's file system. The Merge engine enables us to work around this by joining multiple MyISAM tables together so we can treat the rows as if they were all stored in one large table. Each table that's part of the merged table must share the same column ordering and definitions.

- Memory — The Memory engine stores data in RAM, which gives us lower latency and faster access than disk-based storage can offer. You should only store non-critical data in a Memory-managed table because it will be cleared from RAM when the MySQL server shuts down. Because of its access speed, this engine is useful for storing things like cache or session data.

- NDB — NDB is MySQL's engine designed to support database clustering. Like InnoDB, NDB is also ACID-compliant.

The documentation has more detailed information for each engine[10]. But to help you understand how the engines make different trade-offs to offer better performance or different features, here's a table that highlights some of the key differences between each of them. I've marked features that are dependent upon the engine managing the base table with ?.

Feature	InnoDB	My-ISAM	Archive	Black-hole	CSV	Federated	Merge	Memory	NDB
Storage limit	64TB	256TB	No Limit	N/A	File system	N/A	No Limit	RAM	384EB
ACID	Yes	No	No	No	No	?	No	No	Yes
Foreign keys enforced	Yes	No	No	No	No	?	No	No	Yes
Indexes	Yes	Yes	No	N/A	No	No	Yes	Yes	Yes
Concurrent inserts	Yes	Yes	Yes	Yes	Yes	?	Yes	No	Yes
UNIQUE enforced	Yes	Yes	No	No	No	?	No	Yes	Yes

---

[10] http://dev.mysql.com/doc/refman/5.6/en/storage-engines.html

Fea-ture	Inno-DB	My-ISAM	Ar-chive	Black-hole	CSV	Feder-ated	Merge	Mem-ory	NDB
Full-text search	Yes	Yes	No	N/A	No	?	No	No	No
Lock level	Row	Table	Table	Table	Table	?	Table	Table	Row
Trans-actions	Yes	No	No	No	No	?	No	No	Yes
Spatial data types	Yes	Yes	Yes	Yes	No	?	No	No	Yes
En-crypt-ion	Yes	Yes	Yes	N/A	Yes	Yes	Yes	Yes	Yes
Repli-cation	Yes	Yes	Yes	Yes	Yes	Yes	Yes	Yes	Yes
Clus-tering	No	No	No	No	No	No	No	No	Yes

Adding Data

New rows are added to a table using the INSERT statement. The complexity of an INSERT statement is much less than CREATE TABLE—something you're probably relieved to hear after the last few pages.

Go ahead and issue the following INSERT statement to add a new row of data to the employee table. The statement provides the target table's name, a list of which columns we're supplying data for, and the values themselves.

```
INSERT INTO employee
    (first_name, last_name, email, hire_date)
VALUES
    ('Nischal', 'Bhatia', 'nbhatia@example.com', '2014-12-15');
```

We'll discuss the SELECT statement in the next chapter, but for now we can use the following to look at the contents of the employee table and verify the record was successfully added:

```
SELECT * FROM employee;
```

The reply shown in the command-line client should look like this:

```
+-----------+----------+----------+--------------------+----------+-----+
|employee_id|last_name|first_name|email               |hire_date |notes|
+-----------+----------+----------+--------------------+----------+-----+
|          1|Bhatia   |Nischal   |nbhatia@example.com |2014-12-15|NULL |
+-----------+----------+----------+--------------------+----------+-----+
    1 row in set (0.00 sec)
```

The employee table's CREATE TABLE statement defines six columns, but notice I've only given four in the INSERT statement. The employee_id column was defined with the AUTO_INCREMENT attribute, so MySQL automatically assigns a sequential value for that column. The notes column is assigned NULL indicating the absence of any value. Also notice that I didn't provide the column names in the same order as they appear in the definition. Columns in an INSERT statement can be listed in any order we like so long as the data values are ordered similarly so they match up.

 You Can Omit Column Names

It's possible (but not recommended, if only for reasons of clarity) to omit the column names entirely if you provide values for all of the columns. Without the names, values must be given in the same order that the columns are defined in the CREATE TABLE statement.

```
INSERT INTO employee
VALUES (NULL, 'Bhatia', 'Nischal', 'nbhatia@example.com',
'2014-12-15', NULL);
```

Numeric values, such as INTEGER or DECIMAL values, and the NULL are provided as bare, unquoted literals. Values for the other data types, like CHAR and DATE, are given as quoted strings. MySQL's default configuration allows both single quotes ('…') and double quotes ("…") for this, but single quotes are preferred because then your statements won't rely on a specific configuration.

You may be wondering what happens if a single-quoted string value *contains* a quote mark, as in the name O'Brian. We need to **escape** the quote by adding a designated character before it. This way, MySQL knows the quote doesn't mark the end of the string. The traditional approach is to duplicate the quote, as in 'O''Brian'. By default, MySQL also supports using the backslash character, as in 'O\'Brian'. You can find more information on strings in the documentation[11].

Practice writing some INSERT statements. Try adding a few more rows to the employee table, omitting the employee_id value as we did before, and then retrieve the table's contents to see the auto-incrementing values assigned by MySQL.

Now try adding a row to the address table. Remember, the table's employee_id field was defined as a foreign key that points back to the employee table. This means the employee_id value of Nischal Bhatia's address record must match the employee_id value of his employment record. For me, that value is 1 because it was the first row I added to employee table.

```
INSERT INTO address
    (employee_id, address, city, state, postcode)
VALUES
    (1, '123 Main Street', 'Anytowne', 'XE', '97052');
```

Using Transactions

A **transaction** is a set of statements that are treated as a group. The START TRANSACTION statement begins a transaction and MySQL considers any statements that follow

---

[11] http://dev.mysql.com/doc/refman/5.6/en/string-literals.html

to be part of that transaction. The transaction ends with either a COMMIT or ROLLBACK statement. COMMIT finalizes the transaction, making the changes official, and ROLLBACK rolls back the transaction, discarding any changes.

Let's perform a small experiment using transactions to highlight the ACID concepts of atomicity, consistency, isolation, and durability. First, send the following statements. You'll see a new row added to the employee table, but it's only temporary because we haven't finalized the transaction yet.

```
START TRANSACTION;

INSERT INTO employee
    (employee_id, last_name, first_name, email, hire_date)
VALUES
    (42, 'Virey', 'Gener', 'gvirey@example.com', '2015-04-02');

SELECT * FROM employee;
```

Connect to MySQL with another instance of the command-line client in a different terminal and send the same SELECT statement. You'll see that the row is missing from the result. This shows the transaction we initiated in the first client is isolated from any other connection.

Switch back to the first client and roll back the transaction. The SELECT will then show the row is no longer in the employee table. The rollback has left the data in a consistent state; the same rows that were there before we started the transaction are there and no constraints are violated.

```
ROLLBACK;

SELECT * FROM employee;
```

Let's start another transaction and add some rows, but this time we'll commit it.

```
START TRANSACTION;

INSERT INTO employee
    (employee_id, last_name, first_name, email, hire_date)
VALUES
    (42, 'Virey', 'Gener', 'gvirey@example.com', '2015-04-02');
```

```
INSERT INTO address
    (employee_id, address, city, state, postcode)
VALUES
    (42, '227 North Avenue', 'Anytowne', 'XE', '97052');

COMMIT;
```

Sending a SELECT statement in both clients should show that Gener's details have been finalized in the database. The two INSERT statements were executed as an atomic unit—the effect of the transaction is all or nothing. All of the data was written to the database when we committed the transaction and the only way to update or remove the information is by issuing other statements.

Conclusion

In this chapter, we learned how to define a new database table with the CREATE TABLE statement and how to add rows to a table using INSERT. For CREATE TABLE, we discussed what data types are available with MySQL, how AUTO_INCREMENT instructs MySQL to assign sequential integer values to a primary key, and how each storage engine targets a different usage scenario. For INSERT, we briefly discussed string quoting and experimented using transactions.

Before moving on, take some time to play around with what we've covered here. See what happens when you try to add a row to address with an employee_id value that doesn't exist in the employee table. What happens if you attempt to add a row to the employee table with an employee_id value that's already used? Can you add more than one row with the same employee_id in the address table? If so, then what does this mean about the relationship between the employee and address tables? See hows MySQL responds when you try to store a value that exceeds the limits of its data type.

As the number of rows in a table increases, we'll want something better than the way we've used SELECT so far. The next chapter will discuss how we can retrieve only the data we're interested in. I'll also show you how to update and delete rows. By the end of the Chapter 3, you'll know how to perform the four major operations with MySQL that are expected from any database server: create rows (INSERT), retrieve them (SELECT), update them (UPDATE), and delete them (DELETE).

Chapter 3

Retrieving and Updating Data

In Chapter 2, I briefly introduced you to the SELECT statement by using SELECT *
to display all of the rows in the employee and address tables. But SELECT is certainly
more powerful and flexible than that. It has the ability to retrieve only certain
columns, filter and sort rows, and even select rows from multiple tables based on
the relationships we've defined. You'll learn how to use SELECT to do all that and
more in this chapter and in Chapter 4.

I also promised to show you the UPDATE and DELETE statements so you'll be able to
perform the four basic data operations: creating rows, retrieving them, and keeping
them current either by updating them or deleting them. You already know how to
create rows, so in this chapter we'll discuss retrieval, updating, and deletion.

There's a small bit of housekeeping we need to tend to, however, before we turn
our full attention to writing SELECT, UPDATE, and DELETE statements. The jumpstart
database has served us well so far, but we'd spend a fair amount of time to make it
suitable for experimenting with for the rest of the book. So, first we'll install the
sakila database (named after MySQL's dolphin mascot).

Deploying Sakila

Let's switch from the `jumpstart` database to `sakila`, the standard training database available from MySQL's website. It represents activity at a fictitious DVD rental store and includes customers, inventory, and sales data.

 A Little Bit of History

> Brick-and-mortar video rental outlets have largely been displaced by video on demand and DVD mailing services like Netflix. Take it from me (as someone who's old enough to remember), this wasn't the case in 2005 when the `sakila` database was first developed. The revolution had only just begun, and a mom-and-pop video store could still be found in every neighborhood.

The following steps download the necessary files and sets up the database. As in Chapter 1, if your server isn't running a graphical interface then you'll need to complete the download steps on a separate system and copy the archive over.

1. Open a web browser and navigate to the Other MySQL Documentation page at http://dev.mysql.com/doc/index-other.html .

2. Scroll down to the **Example Databases** section and click on the appropriate download link for the `sakila` database. TGZ is recommended for Linux users and ZIP for Windows users.

3. Navigate to the directory where you downloaded the archive to. Extract its contents and navigate into the new `sakila-db` directory it produces.

   Linux users can execute the following commands:

   ```
   cd /tmp
   gzip -cd sakila-db.tar.gz | tar xvf -
   cd sakila-db
   ```

   Windows users can perform the following steps:

   a. Navigate to the download folder using File Explorer. Right-click the archive and click **Extract All...** to extract its contents.

b. Navigate into the new `sakila-db` folders until you reach the SQL files. Click in File Explorer's address bar to highlight the location and press **CTRL+C** to copy it to your clipboard.

c. Navigate into the folder using Command Prompt. The location stored in the clipboard can be pasted by right-clicking anywhere in the prompt's window and selecting **Paste**.

```
CD "C:\Users\UserName\Downloads\sakila-db"
```

4. The `sakila-schema.sql` file contains the statements necessary to create the database, its tables, and other assets. Execute the following command in the terminal or Command Prompt to import it and provide the password for MySQL's root user when prompted (this was set in Chapter 1).

```
mysql -u root -p < sakila-schema.sql
```

5. Now we need to grant privileges to our "jump" user account so we can use it to access the database. Connect to MySQL using the root account, and issue the following GRANT and FLUSH statements.

```
GRANT CREATE, DROP, ALTER, INSERT, UPDATE, SELECT, DELETE,
INDEX, CREATE VIEW, CREATE ROUTINE, ALTER ROUTINE, EXECUTE,
TRIGGER, INDEX ON sakila.* TO 'jump'@'localhost';
GRANT SUPER, RELOAD, FILE ON *.* TO 'jump'@'localhost';
FLUSH PRIVILEGES;
```

6. Finally, exit the command-line client and execute the following command to populate the `sakila` tables with data from `sakila-data.sql`:

```
mysql -u jump -p < sakila-data.sql
```

 More Privileges

Notice that we specified more privileges than we did the last time we used GRANT. The additional privileges give our account access to functionality we'll need later in the book. Also, notice that two **GRANT** statements are issued—one that references the `sakila` database and another that references *.*. The privileges given in the second **GRANT** statement are global privileges, valid across all databases managed by MySQL (I figured now is as good a time as any to add them).

Take a few minutes to familiarize yourself with the new database. Use the **SHOW TABLES** and **DESCRIBE** or **SHOW CREATE TABLE** statements discussed in Chapter 1 to see what tables exist and what their definitions are.

Retrieving Data

Of course, it wouldn't make sense to place information in a database if we could never pull it back out again. The SQL workhorse statement **SELECT** gives us this ability.

Let's pull some data out of the `actor` table first. The table consists of four columns, `actor_id`, `first_name`, `last_name`, and `last_update`, and holds 200 rows of data. You've already seen that * is used a shorthand notation to retrieve all of the columns, so we'll see how to retrieve only the specific columns we're interested in. Make sure you're connected to MySQL using the "jump" account with `sakila` set as the active database, and then issue this statement:

```
SELECT last_name, first_name FROM actor;
```

The desired columns, in this case `last_name` and `first_name`, are given in the **SELECT** statement as a comma-separated list. MySQL's response looks like this:

```
+--------------+--------------+
| last_name    | first_name   |
+--------------+--------------+
| GUINESS      | PENELOPE     |
| WAHLBERG     | NICK         |
| CHASE        | ED           |
:
| FAWCETT      | JULIA        |
```

```
| TEMPLE       | THORA        |
+--------------+--------------+
200 rows in set (0.00 sec)
```

 Just Showing a Snippet

Imagine all of the paper that would be wasted if I duplicated the entire result set for each example! To save the trees, I've shown just a handful of rows from the beginning and end of the result. A vertical ellipsis represents the omitted rows. You'll see this often throughout the book.

The rows will most likely be returned to us in the same order they were added to the actor table, but this isn't guaranteed. MySQL makes no promises about the order in which it will return the rows if we don't specifically ask for them to be sorted. As long as 200 rows are returned, and you only see values from the last_name and first_name columns, it's okay if your response reflects a different ordering than in the example here.

Ordering Results

When the order of rows in the result is important, we can use an ORDER BY clause in the SELECT statement and MySQL will sort the rows before returning them to us. Reissue the SELECT statement, but this time add ORDER BY to sort the results.

```
SELECT last_name, first_name FROM actor ORDER BY last_name;
```

MySQL sorts the rows in ascending order (A–Z or 1, 2, 3, ...), based on the values in the last_name column, and responds like so:

```
+--------------+--------------+
| last_name    | first_name   |
+--------------+--------------+
| AKROYD       | CHRISTIAN    |
| AKROYD       | KIRSTEN      |
| AKROYD       | DEBBIE       |
:
| ZELLWEGER    | CAMERON      |
```

```
| ZELLWEGER     | JULIA       |
+---------------+-------------+
200 rows in set (0.00 sec)
```

The default sort direction is ascending, but we can explicitly request ascending with the keyword ASC or descending order (Z–A or ..., 3, 2, 1) with DESC. We can also sort the results on multiple columns.

Let's fine-tune the sorting by modifying our statement's ORDER BY clause.

```
SELECT last_name, first_name FROM actor ORDER BY last_name ASC,
first_name DESC;
```

We've asked MySQL to sort the results first by the values in the last_name column, which I've explicitly requested as ascending rather than relying on the default behavior, and then by first_name in descending order. The response we get back looks like this:

```
+---------------+-------------+
| last_name     | first_name  |
+---------------+-------------+
| AKROYD        | KIRSTEN     |
| AKROYD        | DEBBIE      |
| AKROYD        | CHRISTIAN   |
:
| ZELLWEGER     | JULIA       |
| ZELLWEGER     | CAMERON     |
+---------------+-------------+
200 rows in set (0.00 sec)
```

There are only 200 rows in the actor table, so MySQL can fetch them, order them, and return them to us in a fraction of a second. As the number of rows increases, or as the complexity of a SELECT statement grows, the retrieval and sorting processes become slower. Because of this, it's a good idea to make a habit of thinking carefully about the statements you write and retrieving only the data you need.

Ordering is influenced by **character collation**, a set of rules that dictate which character comes before the other when sorting. For example, diacritics are ignored in English, so "Böhm" comes before "Brown". Yet in Swedish, Ö is an independent letter that sorts after R, so "Brown" comes before "Böhm". Also governed by the collation is whether sort comparisons are case-sensitive or not.

The statement SHOW COLLATION will return a list of collations that your installation of MySQL is aware of. The first part of a collation's name is the character set it's designed to work with. Those ending in _ci perform case-insensitive comparisons, those in _cs perform case-insensitive comparisons, and those in _bin use the underlying binary value of each character in comparisons.

```
SHOW COLLATION;

+---------------------+---------+-----+--------+----------+---------+
| Collation           | Charset | Id  | Default| Compiled | Sortlen |
+---------------------+---------+-----+--------+----------+---------+
| big5_chinese_ci     | big5    |   1 | Yes    | Yes      |       1 |
| big5_bin            | big5    | 848 |        | Yes      |       1 |
| dec8_swedish_ci     | dec8    |   3 | Yes    | Yes      |       1 |
:
| eucjpms_japanese_ci | eucjpms |  97 | Yes    | Yes      |       1 |
| eucjpms_bin         | eucjpms |  98 |        | Yes      |       1 |
+---------------------+---------+-----+--------+----------+---------+
219 rows in set (0.00 sec)
```

A yes value in the output's Default column means that collation is the default for its character set. MySQL's default character set is latin1 and the default collation is latin1_swedish_ci (MySQL AB was a Swedish company, after all). The tables in sakila were defined to use utf8, which the default collation for is utf8_general_ci. A different collation can be given in the ORDER BY clause to override the default.

```
SELECT last_name, first_name FROM actor ORDER BY last_name
COLLATE utf8_bin ASC;
```

 ## Character Matters

If you request a collation that wasn't designed to work with a column's character set, MySQL will respond with an error message similar to the following:

```
ERROR 1253 (42000): COLLATION 'latin1_general_cs' is not
valid for CHARACTER SET 'utf8'
```

Character sets and collations are complex topics. If you want to go down the collation rabbit hole, check out the following to learn more:

- MySQL Manual: Globalization[1]

- MySQL's Character Sets and Collations Demystified[2]

- MySQL Tutorial: Setting Character Sets and Collations in MySQL[3]

- Sorting It All Out: an Introduction to Collation[4]

Managing the Number of Returned Rows

We're able to restrict what data we retrieve, in a horizontal sense, by listing specific table columns in a SELECT statement. Restricting in the vertical sense requires us to limit the number of rows we retrieve. There are two ways to accomplish this: selecting rows that match some filtering criteria that we specify, and instructing MySQL to return no more than some maximum number of rows.

The LIMIT clause places a hard limit on the number of rows MySQL returns to us. For example, if we're only interested in the first five actors in the result set, we can add LIMIT 5 to the SELECT statement.

```
SELECT last_name, first_name FROM actor ORDER BY last_name,
first_name DESC LIMIT 5;
```

MySQL still sorts all of the rows, but then simply "chops off" the first five rows and sends those back to us.

---

[1] http://dev.mysql.com/doc/refman/5.6/en/globalization.html

[2] http://code.openark.org/blog/mysql/mysqls-character-sets-and-collations-demystified

[3] http://www.mysqltutorial.org/mysql-collation

[4] http://download.microsoft.com/download/3/7/1/371c04e1-1fc3-462c-abbc-fa6068e14643/21-Collation-Intro.pdf

```
+-------------+-------------+
| last_name   | first_name  |
+-------------+-------------+
| AKROYD      | KIRSTEN     |
| AKROYD      | DEBBIE      |
| AKROYD      | CHRISTIAN   |
| ALLEN       | MERYL       |
| ALLEN       | KIM         |
+-------------+-------------+
5 rows in set (0.10 sec)
```

 ### Clause Ordering

The order in which clauses appear in a SELECT statement is important, but don't worry if you can't always remember the correct order. You can always consult the documentation for SELECT[5]. After a while, writing clauses in the necessary order will become second nature to you.

The WHERE clause gives us the ability to specify conditions that a row must match for MySQL to include it in the results. For example, we can retrieve only the rows with a column value greater or less than some arbitrary value we provide. Let's look at some data from the film table:

```
SELECT title, length, rating FROM film WHERE length < 60
ORDER BY title;
```

The statement retrieves a movie's title, running time, and rating for each row. The table's length column holds the movie's duration in minutes, so the WHERE clause specified the condition as length < 60. The result should only show the rows for movies with a run time less than 60 minutes.

```
+------------------------+--------+--------+
| title                  | length | rating |
+------------------------+--------+--------+
| ACE GOLDFINGER         |     48 | G      |
| ADAPTATION HOLES       |     50 | NC-17  |
| AIRPORT POLLOCK        |     54 | R      |
:
```

---

[5] http://dev.mysql.com/doc/refman/5.6/en/select.html

```
| WOLVES DESIRE          |      55 | NC-17 |
| ZORRO ARK              |      50 | NC-17 |
+-----------------------+--------+--------+
96 rows in set (0.00 sec)
```

Every condition we write needs to accurately reflect what we want to retrieve because MySQL will follow it to the letter. I retrieved the movies that run *less than* an hour. But what about those that run exactly 60 minutes? To include them, I need to update the WHERE condition to read length <= 60. To retrieve the movies that run exactly 60 minutes, I'd update the condition to read length = 60.

We can also use standard logical operators like AND and OR to provide multiple conditions. For example, to select movies that run between one hour and two hours inclusively, we can specify two conditions and use the AND operator.

```
SELECT title, length, rating FROM film WHERE length >= 60 AND
length <= 120 ORDER BY title;

+-------------------------------+--------+--------+
| title                         | length | rating |
+-------------------------------+--------+--------+
| ACADEMY DINOSAUR              |     86 | PG     |
| AFFAIR PREJUDICE              |    117 | G      |
| AIRPLANE SIERRA               |     62 | PG-13  |
:
| ZHIVAGO CORE                  |    105 | PG-13  |
| ZOOLANDER FICTION             |    101 | NC-17  |
+-------------------------------+--------+--------+
447 rows in set (0.00 sec)
```

To select those that run exactly one, two, or three hours, we can provide conditions using the OR operator.

```
SELECT title, length FROM film WHERE length = 60 OR length = 120 OR
length = 180 ORDER BY title;

+-------------------------------+--------+--------+
| title                         | length | rating |
+-------------------------------+--------+--------+
| ALLEY EVOLUTION               |    180 | NC-17  |
| BUBBLE GROSSE                 |     60 | R      |
| CALENDAR GUNFIGHT             |    120 | NC-17  |
```

```
 :
| SOMETHING DUCK            |    180 | NC-17 |
| UNTOUCHABLES SUNRISE      |    120 | NC-17 |
+--------------------------+--------+--------+
24 rows in set (0.00 sec)
```

These examples demonstrate what a SELECT statement looks like with more than one condition in its WHERE clause, but they also highlight two very common scenarios. Specifying that a column's value must be within a certain range, or be equal to one of several allowed values, is so common that there are special operators for these tasks: BETWEEN … AND and IN. The condition length BETWEEN 60 AND 120 has the same meaning as length >= 60 AND length <= 120 and the condition length IN (60, 120, 180) has the same meaning as length = 60 OR length = 120 OR length = 180. The IN operator is especially helpful for keeping statements short and readable when the WHERE clause would otherwise become unwieldy with many different comparison values.

We can use the = operator to match an entire string value, as with title = 'HOLIDAY GAMES', but sometimes we'll only know a portion of the string. In such cases, we can use the LIKE operator with the wild cards % and _, like this:

```
SELECT title, length, rating FROM film WHERE title LIKE '%GAME%'
ORDER BY title;
```

_ matches a single character in the string and % matches any number of characters, so the above statement returns all the movies with GAME somewhere in their title. The results are:

```
+------------------+--------+--------+
| title            | length | rating |
+------------------+--------+--------+
| GAMES BOWFINGER  |    119 | PG-13  |
| HOLIDAY GAMES    |     78 | PG-13  |
| RAGE GAMES       |    120 | R      |
+------------------+--------+--------+
3 rows in set (0.00 sec)
```

For the sake of convenience, here's a table that shows some of the basic comparison operators available to us. More information can be found in the online documentation[6]. Other operators are discussed in the documentation as well, like the standard mathematical operators +, -, *, /, and %, and the logical operators AND, OR, NOT, and XOR.

Operator	Description
A = B	True when A and B are equal
A < B	True when A is less than B
A <= B	True when A equal or less than B
A > B	True when A is greater than B
A >= B	True when A equal or greater than B
A != B or A <> B	True when A and B are not equal
A IS NULL	True when A is a NULL value
A LIKE 'PATTERN%'	True when A matches the pattern string (pattern wildcards are % and _)
A REGEXP '/EXPRESSION/'	True when A matches the regular expression
A BETWEEN B AND C	True when A is in the range of B and C inclusive (same as A >= B AND A <= C)
A IN (B,C,D)	True when A is equal to one of the values in the given set (same as A = B OR A = C OR A = D)

It's also possible to combine the results from multiple SELECT statements using UNION. Because each additional set is appended to the result, each statement must return the same number of columns.

```
SELECT title FROM film WHERE title LIKE 'A%'
UNION
SELECT title FROM film WHERE title LIKE 'Z%';

+-----------------------+
| title                 |
+-----------------------+
```

---

[6] http://dev.mysql.com/doc/refman/5.6/en/non-typed-operators.html

```
|  ACADEMY DINOSAUR      |
|  ACE GOLDFINGER        |
|  ADAPTATION HOLES      |
 :
|  ZHIVAGO CORE          |
|  ZOOLANDER FICTION     |
+------------------------+
49 rows in set (0.00 sec)
```

Aggregate Functions and Grouping

Aside from filtering and sorting, MySQL also has the ability to group and condense rows and summarize their data. Aggregate functions like COUNT(), SUM(), and MAX() perform their calculation using all of the column's values from the matching rows to come up with a single summary value.

```
SELECT MAX(amount) FROM payment;

+-------------+
| MAX(amount) |
+-------------+
|       11.99 |
+-------------+
1 row in set (0.01 sec)
```

As its name suggests, MAX() returns the largest value from all of its rows. In the example above, it's using all of the amount values in the payment table to show us that the most money any customer has spent in one visit to the store is $11.99.

The COUNT() function simply counts the number of rows it passes over. For this reason, it's quite common to use COUNT() to determine the size of a table.

```
SELECT COUNT(payment_id) FROM payment;
```

MySQL reports back that there are over 16,000 rows in the payment table.

```
+-------------------+
| COUNT(payment_id) |
+-------------------+
```

```
|               16017 |
+--------------------+
1 row in set (0.01 sec)
```

Aggregate functions are most useful when rows are broken up into groups. The calculation is performed using each row in the group, and we can draw comparisons based on the differences between groups to gain better insight into our data. The GROUP BY clause gathers the rows into groups.

Suppose we want to find the top 10 customers who've spent the most money renting movies. We could issue several SELECT statements to retrieve the necessary data and perform the calculations manually, but it's faster and easier to ask MySQL to do the work for us.

```
SELECT customer_id, SUM(amount) AS amt FROM payment GROUP BY
customer_id ORDER BY amt DESC LIMIT 10;
```

The GROUP BY clause batches rows with the same customer_id values into groups. Then, the SUM() function adds up the values and returns the sum for each group. By gathering the rows into a different batch for each customer and summing their payment amounts, we can easily work out how much each customer has spent. Sorting the results and returning the 10 highest values shows us who our most profitable customers are.

```
+-------------+--------+
| customer_id | amt    |
+-------------+--------+
|         526 | 221.55 |
|         148 | 216.54 |
|         144 | 195.58 |
|         178 | 194.61 |
|         137 | 194.61 |
|         459 | 186.62 |
|         469 | 177.60 |
|         468 | 175.61 |
|         236 | 175.58 |
```

```
|           181 | 174.66 |
+---------------+--------+
10 rows in set (0.01 sec)
```

The AS Keyword

The AS keyword creates a temporary alias for a column or expression. Rather than writing ORDER BY SUM(amount) DESC in the example, I gave the value the alias amt.

Keeping Data Fresh

Now we'll look at the UPDATE and DELETE statements. Just like SELECT, UPDATE and DELETE rely on a WHERE clause to target specific rows. If such a clause is absent, the statements affect every row in the table (behavior we generally won't want).

Use With Caution

UPDATE and DELETE are potentially dangerous statements because they will update or delete the wrong rows if the WHERE clause doesn't match what you intend—a situation you may not be able to recover from without a current backup on hand. I recommend that you write a SELECT statement to verify the conditions in your WHERE clause first to be sure you match the intended rows before issuing a destructive statement.

Updating Data

Suppose a customer recently married her long-time sweetheart (aww!), changed her name from Courtney Day to Courtney Day-Webb, and we've been tasked with updating her details in the customer table. We'll start by retrieving her current details with a WHERE clause to match her maiden name.

```
SELECT customer_id, first_name, last_name FROM customer WHERE
first_name = 'Courtney' AND last_name = 'Day';
```

Courtney's name is distinct enough that only one row matches. MySQL returns the following:

```
+---------------+-------------+-----------+---------------------+
| customer_id   | first_name  | last_name | last_update         |
+---------------+-------------+-----------+---------------------+
|           245 | COURTNEY    | DAY       | 2006-02-15 04:57:20 |
+---------------+-------------+-----------+---------------------+
1 row in set (0.00 sec)
```

If multiple rows were returned, we'd need to decide which is the correct row to update and what unique values we could use to target it. A table's primary key is typically a good choice in this situation, because the values in such columns must be unique across all of rows in in the table. The customer_id column is the customer table's primary key, so WHERE customer_id = 245 unambiguously identifies the target row.

To update Courtney's last name, we'll send MySQL the following UPDATE statement:

```
UPDATE customer SET last_name = 'DAY-WEBB' WHERE
customer_id = 245;
```

MySQL reports back that the row has been updated. And if we select the row again, we can see this for ourselves.

```
+---------------+-------------+-----------+---------------------+
| customer_id   | first_name  | last_name | last_update         |
+---------------+-------------+-----------+---------------------+
|           245 | COURTNEY    | DAY-WEBB  | 2015-03-16 13:27:44 |
+---------------+-------------+-----------+---------------------+
1 row in set (0.00 sec)
```

If you compare these values with the ones MySQL retrieved for our first SELECT statement, you'll notice the value of the last_update column has changed as well. The column is defined in the customer table's CREATE TABLE statement as TIMESTAMP. As you may recall from the discussion in Chapter 2, MySQL updates a TIMESTAMP column's value whenever any of the values in the row are updated.

If you don't want a TIMESTAMP value to change when you modify another value, you need to specify that in the UPDATE statement as well, like so:

```
UPDATE customer SET last_name = 'DAY-WEBB', last_update =
last_update WHERE customer_id = 245;
```

This example UPDATE statement also illustrates a couple interesting points: we can provide as many comma-separated column assignments as we like after the SET keyword, and MySQL uses the column's value of the row whenever the column name appears on the right-hand side in an expression.

Deleting Data

A common practice when deleting data is to perform a **soft delete**—that is, not to delete a row, but rather to toggle the value in a dedicated column that represents whether the row is considered live. The customer table defines a TINYINT column named active for this purpose. A drawback to this approach is that you must remember to provide a WHERE clause with active = 1 with each SELECT statement you write to exclude inactive rows. Another is that unwanted data still resides in the table, taking up storage space and possibly slowing down searches. But on the other hand, this approach makes it possible to recover from accidental deletions simply by toggling the active value back again, something that's not possible with a true deletion.

Useful Info

To set Courtney's row inactive, update the active column to be 0.

```
UPDATE customer SET active = 0 WHERE customer_id = 245;
```

Deleting Inactive Rows

To mitigate the resource consumption issues with soft deletion, one suggestion is to set up a recurring task that deletes inactive rows after a certain amount of time, or to move them to an archive table if the data is still needed (for example, for historical reporting purposes). This can be accomplished using "temporal triggers" which are discussed in Chapter 6.

The DELETE statement permanently deletes matching rows, and looks like this:

```
DELETE FROM customer WHERE customer_id = 245;
```

Aside from being the `customer` table's primary key, the `customer_id` column is also the target of foreign key constraint in the `payment` and `rental` tables. Because of this, the `DELETE` statement above fails if you try to send it with the following error:

```
ERROR 1451 (23000): Cannot delete or update a parent row: a foreign
key constraint fails (`sakila`.`payment`, CONSTRAINT
`fk_payment_customer` FOREIGN KEY (`customer_id`) REFERENCES
`customer` (`customer_id`) ON UPDATE CASCADE)
```

MySQL knows there are rows in the `payment` table related to the row in the `customer` table, and deleting the customer row would leave those rows orphaned, so the foreign key constraint is enforced to preserve the integrity of our data. The same situation would occur if we were to delete a row from the `employee` table in the `jumpstart` database: any corresponding rows in the `address` table would be left orphaned.

There must be no dependent rows elsewhere to successfully delete a row targeted by a foreign key constraint, so we need to delete Courtney's payment and rental history (any rows in the `payment` and `rental` tables with a `customer_id` value of 245) before we are allowed to remove her `customer` row.

```
DELETE FROM payment WHERE customer_id = 245;
DELETE FROM rental WHERE customer_id = 245;
DELETE FROM customer WHERE customer_id = 245;
```

 Cascading Actions

When defining relationships, we can specify `ON DELETE CASCADE` as part of the definition of a table's foreign key. Then, whenever MySQL detects the delete action would result in orphaned rows, the delete will cascade to the associated table and those rows will be deleted as well. The documentation offers more information on `ON DELETE CASCADE` and other cascading behavior for foreign keys[7].

---

[7] http://dev.mysql.com/doc/refman/5.6/en/create-table-foreign-keys.html

Conclusion

In this chapter, we switched from the jumpstart database to sakila and learned how to retrieve data, sort it, and summarize it with SELECT and its various clauses. We also learned how to keep data up to date using UPDATE, and how to delete stale data using either a soft deletion strategy or DELETE statements. There's no denying we've covered a lot.

To reinforce what you've learned here and gain more insight, see what the MySQL documentation has to say about SELECT, UPDATE, and DELETE. Also, look up the operators used in WHERE clauses, GROUP BY, and aggregate functions. Then take some time to play around with the topics we discussed here. Retrieve all of the actors with "SON" in their last name and sort them alphabetically. Calculate how many films there are for each rating category—G, PG, PG-13, R, and NC-17. What's the ID of the customer who's made the most visits to the video store?

In the next chapter, we'll work more with SELECT. You'll see how to use multiple tables in the same statement and how the complexity of such statements can be abstracted by virtual tables called views. I'll also introduce you to normalization, a process that keeps our table relationships healthy and protects the integrity of our data.

Chapter 4

Working with Multiple Tables

Next to the table, the most important concept in the world of relational databases is, not surprisingly, relationships. Very early on in our discussions you saw how a record can be organized across multiple tables—each row in a table being part of a larger whole. It follows, then, that you'll sometimes find the need to work with several tables at the same time.

This chapter is all about working with multiple tables. In it's first half, we'll continue with SELECT, and you'll learn how to reference more than one table in the same statement. I'll show you why this is useful and the different ways the tables can be combined. Depending on the number of tables and how they are related, things can start to get a bit unwieldy. To help combat this, we'll also take a look at how to define and use virtual tables known as views.

In the second half of this chapter, we'll shift our attention to maintaining happy and healthy relationships. You'll learn about **normalization**, the practice of organizing tables to minimize redundancy and to promote data consistency and integrity. Then I'll introduce you to ALTER TABLE, the statement which modifies an existing table (something that comes in handy when normalizing a database).

This chapter also brings an end to our discussions concerning basic SQL. The rest of the book will focus on more MySQL-specific topics, like communicating with a MySQL server from code, programming the database, and making backups.

Joining Tables

Let's identify the top five actors who made the most film appearances and the number of films they've each starred in. Using what we've learned so far, we'll need to write two `SELECT` statements. The first statement will target the `film_actor` table which contains a row for each actor's appearance in a film.

```
SELECT actor_id, COUNT(actor_id) AS appearances
FROM film_actor GROUP BY actor_id ORDER BY appearances DESC
LIMIT 5;
```

The statement groups the results using the `actor_id` and the `COUNT()` function gives us the number of rows in each group. By ordering the results and looking at the first five rows, we're able to determine the IDs and number of appearances for each of the most active actors. The response looks like this:

```
+-----------+-------------+
| actor_id  | appearances |
+-----------+-------------+
|       107 |          42 |
|       102 |          41 |
|       198 |          40 |
|       181 |          39 |
|        23 |          37 |
+-----------+-------------+
5 rows in set (0.01 sec)
```

The actor IDs will be used in our second statement. It maps the IDs to the corresponding rows in the `actor` table so we can retrieve the names.

```
SELECT actor_id, first_name, last_name FROM actor WHERE
actor_id IN (107, 102, 198, 181, 23);
```

Here's the result:

```
+-----------+-------------+-----------+
| actor_id  | first_name  | last_name |
+-----------+-------------+-----------+
|        23 | SANDRA      | KILMER    |
|       102 | WALTER      | TORN      |
|       107 | GINA        | DEGENERES |
|       181 | MATTHEW     | CARREY    |
|       198 | MARY        | KEITEL    |
+-----------+-------------+-----------+
5 rows in set (0.00 sec)
```

We have all the information we wanted, but unfortunately we still need to match up the actors' names and appearance counts manually. This approach has proven less than ideal. If only we had the ability to link the film_actor and actor tables together and perform the operations on their combined rows. Then we could write just one statement, and even get a better result! Well, JOIN lets us do exactly that by connecting two or more tables based on a relationship that we specify.

Here's a SELECT statement that retrieves the names and appearance counts using JOIN (I've added some line breaks and indentation to make the statement easier to read):

```
SELECT
    a.first_name, a.last_name,
    COUNT(fa.film_id) AS appearance_count
FROM
    film_actor AS fa
    JOIN actor AS a ON a.actor_id = fa.actor_id
GROUP BY
    fa.actor_id
ORDER BY
    appearance_count DESC,
    a.first_name ASC,
    a.last_name ASC
LIMIT 5;
```

The result is much better. The rows are sorted, and best of all there's no manual activity required.

```
+-------------+-------------+-------------------+
| first_name  | last_name   | appearance_count  |
+-------------+-------------+-------------------+
| GINA        | DEGENERES   |                42 |
| WALTER      | TORN        |                41 |
| MARY        | KEITEL      |                40 |
| MATTHEW     | CARREY      |                39 |
| SANDRA      | KILMER      |                37 |
+-------------+-------------+-------------------+
5 rows in set (0.00 sec)
```

JOIN pairs the rows of the two tables using the common values in their `actor_id` columns. Which tables, and how rows match up to one another, is up to us. We can join two tables using columns that define a foreign key relationship as we did here, or we can write more interesting joins that join a table against itself. How and what we join depends on the table definitions and the result we're looking to achieve.

Using the AS Keyword

The AS keyword is optional when you define a column or table alias. I typically don't use AS to alias table names in my own day-to-day statements, but I'm using it here for clarity. Regardless, I always use AS with column names because it helps me make sure my column names are correctly separated by commas. Consider the following:

```
SELECT actor_id, first_name last_name FROM actor;
```

It's not clear to someone else looking at the statement whether I'm missing a comma between `first_name` and `last_name` or foolishly aliasing `first_name` in my result set (MySQL will interpret it the second way). Following such conventions makes the intent clear, and thus we know the statement has an error.

Theta-style Joins

The conditions that define the join originally appeared in the statement's WHERE clause, a style now known as **theta-style joins** or **traditional joins**. A theta-style join looks like this:

```
SELECT
    a.first_name, a.last_name,
    COUNT(fa.film_id) AS appearance_count
FROM
    film_actor AS fa
    JOIN actor AS a
WHERE
    a.actor_id = fa.actor_id;
```

Nowadays, most people prefer to write **ANSI-style joins**, which move the conditions into the FROM clause. I've found this style to be easier to understand and easier to debug because the join and filtering conditions aren't muddled together. This is the style I use in this book.

Types of Joins

The three join types available to us with MySQL are INNER JOIN, LEFT OUTER JOIN, and RIGHT OUTER JOIN. The default is INNER JOIN, so when JOIN appears by itself (as it did in the earlier statements) MySQL interprets it as an INNER JOIN. It's important to know how each type behaves because if the desired rows aren't captured by the join in the first place then they can't possibly appear in the final result.

It'll be easier to understand the different joins using two simple tables—each populated with a couple rows of data—than using the actor and film data, so go ahead and set up the tables foo and bar with the following statements:

```
CREATE TABLE foo (
    foo_id INTEGER,
    foo_value CHAR(3)
);

CREATE TABLE bar (
    bar_id INTEGER,
    bar_value CHAR(3),
    foo_id INTEGER
);

INSERT INTO foo (foo_id, foo_value) VALUES (1, 'foo');
INSERT INTO foo (foo_id, foo_value) VALUES (2, 'bar');
```

```
INSERT INTO bar (bar_id, bar_value, foo_id) VALUES (1, 'baz', 2);
INSERT INTO bar (bar_id, bar_value, foo_id) VALUES (2, 'qux', 3);
```

Now let's join the two tables using INNER JOIN.

```
SELECT * FROM foo f INNER JOIN bar b ON b.foo_id = f.foo_id;
```

MySQL compares each row in the first table against each in the second table and identifies matching pairs based on the ON condition. The rows that match are joined together and included in the result. Our ON condition specifies that the value in both tables' foo_id column must be equal, and only one pair of rows meets the requirement.

```
+---------+-----------+---------+-----------+---------+
| foo_id  | foo_value | bar_id  | bar_value | foo_id  |
+---------+-----------+---------+-----------+---------+
|       2 | bar       |       1 | baz       |       2 |
+---------+-----------+---------+-----------+---------+
1 row in set (0.00 sec)
```

It can be helpful to think of the tables in a join as circles in a Venn diagram where the ON condition determines where they intersect. Presented as such, INNER JOIN produces a result that looks like Figure 4.1. The diagonal hatching represents the result of the join.

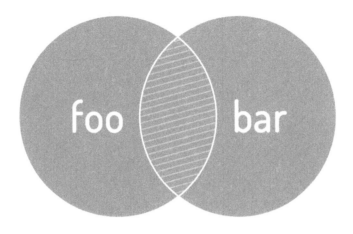

foo **JOIN** bar
foo **INNER JOIN** bar

Figure 4.1. INNER JOIN behavior illustrated as a Venn diagram.

The two OUTER JOINs return the same rows as INNER JOIN, but also include the unmatched rows from one table or the other (the outer parts of the intersecting circles). LEFT OUTER JOIN includes the unmatched rows from the table that appears to the left of the JOIN keyword. In the result, the columns defined by the other table contain NULL.

```
SELECT * FROM foo f LEFT OUTER JOIN bar b ON
f.foo_id = b.foo_id;
+--------+-----------+--------+-----------+--------+
| foo_id | foo_value | bar_id | bar_value | foo_id |
+--------+-----------+--------+-----------+--------+
|      2 | bar       |      1 | baz       |      2 |
|      1 | foo       |   NULL | NULL      |   NULL |
+--------+-----------+--------+-----------+--------+
```

The LEFT OUTER JOIN produces a result that looks like Figure 4.2.

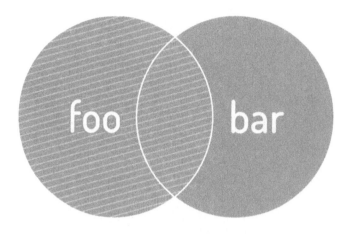

foo LEFT OUTER JOIN bar

Figure 4.2. LEFT OUTER JOIN behavior illustrated as a Venn diagram.

 NULL is Different

Remember that NULL is a special value that represents the absence of a value. NULLs are treated differently from other values, and any comparisons that involve NULLs will themselves return NULL. This means operators like = or != don't work with filtering NULLs. Be sure you use IS NULL and IS NOT NULL when checking for NULLs. More information can be found in the online documentation[1].

RIGHT OUTER JOIN is the opposite of LEFT OUTER JOIN, returning the unmatched rows from the table appearing to the right of the JOIN keyword.

```
SELECT * FROM foo f RIGHT OUTER JOIN bar b ON
f.foo_id = b.foo_id;
+--------+-----------+--------+-----------+--------+
| foo_id | foo_value | bar_id | bar_value | foo_id |
+--------+-----------+--------+-----------+--------+
|      2 | bar       |      1 | baz       |      2 |
```

---

[1] http://dev.mysql.com/doc/refman/5.6/en/problems-with-null.html

```
|   NULL | NULL        |        2 | qux         |        3 |
+--------+-------------+----------+-------------+---------+
2 rows in set (0.00 sec)
```

Figure 4.3 shows the diagram for `RIGHT OUTER JOIN`.

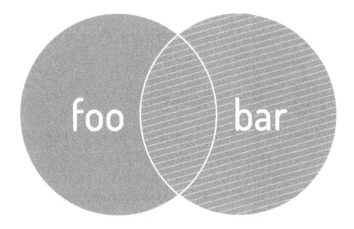

foo **RIGHT OUTER JOIN** bar

Figure 4.3. `RIGHT OUTTER JOIN` behavior illustrated as a Venn diagram.

When no condition is specified for how the tables should be joined, MySQL matchs
every row in the first table against every row in the second. This is what's known
as a **Cartesian product**. Generally, this is something to avoid because the number
of rows in the the result set will be quite large.

```
SELECT * FROM foo JOIN bar;
+--------+-----------+--------+-----------+--------+
| foo_id | foo_value | bar_id | bar_value | foo_id |
+--------+-----------+--------+-----------+--------+
|      1 | foo       |      1 | baz       |      2 |
|      2 | bar       |      1 | baz       |      2 |
|      1 | foo       |      2 | qux       |      3 |
```

```
|        2 | bar       |        2 | qux       |        3 |
+----------+-----------+----------+-----------+----------+
4 rows in set (0.00 sec)
```

No FULL OUTER JOIN

Unlike some other relational database systems, MySQL does not support FULL OUTER JOIN—a join that includes the unmatched rows of both the left and right tables. See the post "How to Simulate FULL OUTER JOIN in MySQL"[2] by Baron Schwartz.

Abstracting with Views

Many everyday objects are made up of smaller components that are assembled together. For example, a computer is built from various parts, one of which is the motherboard. The motherboard in turn has circuits built using integrated chips, transistors, resistors, and capacitors. Each level of abstraction hides the underlying complexity beneath it. This allows us to think of the components as building blocks; we can combine them in different ways to build new products without concerning ourselves with minor implementation details.

Views give us a way to abstract a complex statement by presenting its result as a virtual table, thus hiding any potentially complex joins, calculations, and filtering operations from other statements that reference it. Views look like regular tables to our SELECT statements, and we can even join multiple views if we want, although the data is still stored in their original base tables.

Here's a CREATE VIEW statement that abstracts our earlier join and grouping to find how many film appearances each actor has made:

```
CREATE VIEW actor_appearance
AS SELECT
    a.first_name, a.last_name,
    COUNT(fa.film_id) AS appearance_count
FROM
    film_actor AS fa
```

---

[2] http://www.xaprb.com/blog/2006/05/26/how-to-write-full-outer-join-in-mysql/

```
    JOIN actor AS a ON a.actor_id = fa.actor_id
GROUP BY
    fa.actor_id;
```

We can now easily identify the actors with the most appearances with a concise and easy-to-understand statement:

```
SELECT * FROM actor_appearance ORDER BY appearance_count
DESC LIMIT 5;
```

The column names of a view are the names that result from the underlying statement. That is, if the SELECT statement retrieves the actor_id, first_name, and last_name columns, those will be the names of the view's columns. This can sometimes be problematic because column names must be unique.

Suppose we want a view that presents name and address information from the customer and address tables. Furthermore, let's suppose we want to include the last_update values from both tables. Here's the SELECT statement:

```
SELECT
    c.first_name, c.last_name, c.last_update, a.address,
    a.last_update
FROM
    customer AS c
    JOIN address AS a ON a.address_id = c.address_id;
```

The resulting column names will be first_name, last_name, last_update, address, and last_update. This is fine for a standard SELECT statement, but MySQL will respond with an error if we try to create a view using it because the name last_update is not unique.

```
Error 1060 (42S21): Duplicate column name 'last_name'
```

One solution is to alias the offending column names in the SELECT statement using AS—just as we did earlier to provide more friendly names for calculated columns. Another solution is to explicitly define names for the columns as part of the CREATE VIEW statement. When we do this, the names are placed after the view name and the number of names must match the number of columns returned by the SELECT.

```
CREATE VIEW customer_address (
    first_name, last_name, cust_last_update, address,
    addr_last_upate
)
AS SELECT
    c.first_name, c.last_name, c.last_update, a.address,
    a.last_update
FROM
    customer AS c
    JOIN address AS a ON a.address_id = c.address_id;
```

 Fixing a View

The definition of a view is static. If an identifier referenced in the definition changes—for example, if we rename a table or delete a column—the view will break. You can use ALTER VIEW to redefine the view when this happens.

```
ALTER VIEW customer_address AS SELECT …
```

Aside from helping to reign in complexity, views can provide a certain level of security and peace of mind. Let's revisit the soft delete strategy we talked about in Chapter 3 which uses a dedicated column to specify whether a row is considered active or not. We can define a view that mirrors such tables and filters out the inactive rows.

```
CREATE VIEW active_customer
AS SELECT
    customer_id, first_name, last_name, email
FROM
    customer
WHERE
    active = 1;
```

We can then restrict users to the active_customer view instead of allowing them access to the customer table. They'll only see the active rows while other processes can still access the original data for maintenance and reporting purposes.

We can also restrict what columns a user sees with a view. Notice in the example above that I didn't include the address_id column and a few others. Suppose there's an employee who needs access to the customers' email addresses but not their mailing addresses. The view makes sure only the appropriate information is available without the need for us to redesign the tables.

However, keep in mind that abstracting complexity with views also abstracts the cost of the statement. When working with a view, a user may not be aware of what MySQL is doing behind the scenes, and thus may not understand the true cost in terms of database load caused by the underlying statements.

 Updating View Data

Views behave like regular tables for **SELECT** statements, but not for **UPDATE** and **DELETE** statements. There are many obstacles for MySQL to overcome to be able to mutate the data safely and reliably, so my advice is not to even bother. It's just not worth the hassle. This is because a view is only a definition; the data one returns still lives in the original tables. See the documentation for more information on what affects the updatability of a view[3].

Normal Forms

Armed with the knowledge of how to join tables and abstract complexity behind views, you should never be intimidated by the number of tables in aa normalized database. The term **normalization** refers to the process of organizing data—by following specific rules—to eliminate redundancy and inconsistencies.

The main benefits of database normalization are:

 Decreased storage requirements — duplicate data means there is more data to be stored, which requires more disk space and memory. Minimizing such redundancy makes efficient use of the resources available to the database.

 Data integrity — if the same data appears in several places, there's increased opportunity for inconsistencies to be introduced. For example, if a name appears in two different tables, it's possible to misspell one of the instances or perhaps update one instance and miss the other.

---

[3] http://dev.mysql.com/doc/refman/5.6/en/view-updatability.html

■ Maintainability — the rules for normalization focus on maintaining relationships and put the R in RDBMS. The result is tables that have a clearly defined and logical purpose. When one table stores actor details and another stores movie data, it's easier to update the data than if it were all mixed together in a single table.

A normalized database may be a well-designed database, but you should know that normalization can also have a negative impact on performance. It requires time and effort for MySQL to join tables. We can mitigate this by defining and using keys and indexes properly, and by filtering results so that MySQL is doing the hardest work on the smallest possible number of rows.

There are several levels of normalization. A table is said to be in a specific **normal form** when its tables adhere to that level's rules. I'll keep our discussion here focused on the First Normal Form, Second Normal Form, and Third Normal Form, abbreviated as 1NF, 2NF, and 3NF. Most of the other forms define things that are already a consequence of adhering to these first three forms.

First Normal Form

First Normal Form is simple and pretty much states that every field should hold only one value. Some RDBMSs support compound data types like arrays, but MySQL doesn't. This fortunately goes a long way in helping us avoid breaking this rule. What's left for us to worry about is to avoid using the `SET` data type or any cute hacks designed to cram more than one value into a field, like storing JSON-encoded objects or strings of comma-separated values.

Here's a table that stores some actors and the movies they starred in. Some rows contain more than one movie title in the `film_title` column, violating 1NF.

```
+------------+-----------+-----------------------------+
| first_name | last_name | film_title                  |
+------------+-----------+-----------------------------+
| SCARLETT   | BENING    | ROOF CHAMPION, YOUTH KICK    |
| MICHAEL    | BOLGER    | HOMEWARD CIDER, SANTA PARIS  |
```

```
| VAL        | BOLGER    | PATIENT SISTER, YOUTH KICK |
| DARYL      | CRAWFORD  | BROTHERHOOD BLANKET        |
+------------+-----------+----------------------------+
```

To fix this situation, we need to split up the offending values and place them in their own rows. The `first_name` and `last_name` values are duplicated so each row is complete.

```
+------------+-----------+---------------------+
| first_name | last_name | film_title          |
+------------+-----------+---------------------+
| SCARLETT   | BENING    | ROOF CHAMPION       |
| SCARLETT   | BENING    | YOUTH KICK          |
| MICHAEL    | BOLGER    | HOMEWARD CIDER      |
| MICHAEL    | BOLGER    | SANTA PARIS         |
| VAL        | BOLGER    | PATIENT SISTER      |
| VAL        | BOLGER    | YOUTH KICK          |
| DARYL      | CRAWFORD  | BROTHERHOOD BLANKET |
+------------+-----------+---------------------+
```

The table now meets 1NF because every field holds a single value. No field contains multiple values.

Second Normal Form

A table is in Second Normal Form when it meets the criteria for 1NF (so all 2NF tables are also 1NF) and every non-key field can be accessed using a logically related key. If the key is a compound key, each field that makes up the key must be related to all of the columns in the row.

Here I've added an `actor_id` column and `film_id` column to the example table which give us a compound key we can use to target an appearance:

```
+----------+------------+-----------+---------+---------------------+
| actor_id | first_name | last_name | film_id | film_title          |
+----------+------------+-----------+---------+---------------------+
|      124 | SCARLETT   | BENING    |     742 | ROOF CHAMPION       |
|      124 | SCARLETT   | BENING    |     997 | YOUTH KICK          |
|      185 | MICHAEL    | BOLGER    |     427 | HOMEWARD CIDER      |
|      185 | MICHAEL    | BOLGER    |     761 | SANTA PARIS         |
|       37 | VAL        | BOLGER    |     663 | PATIENT SISTER      |
```

```
|        37 | VAL         | BOLGER      |        997 | YOUTH KICK          |
|       129 | DARYL       | CRAWFORD    |        101 | BROTHERHOOD BLANKET |
+-----------+-------------+-------------+-----------+---------------------+
```

Focusing on the `film_title` columns, the field in the row with `actor_id` value 124 and `film_id` value 997 holds a different "Youth Kick" string from the row with `actor_id` 37 and `film_id` 997. We can differentiate between them using the `actor_id` and `film_id` values together as a compound key, but the table isn't in 2NF because relying on anything that's not film-related to access a film title is a violation of the rules. That is, there's a logical connection between `film_id` and `film_title` because they both pertain to movies, but `actor_id` has no connection to `film_title`. 2NF's focus is on making sure our keys make logical sense.

The remedy is to move the `film_title` column to its own table.

```
+-----------+-------------+-------------+-----------+
| actor_id  | first_name  | last_name   | film_id   |
+-----------+-------------+-------------+-----------+
|       124 | SCARLETT    | BENING      |       742 |
|       124 | SCARLETT    | BENING      |       997 |
|       185 | MICHAEL     | BOLGER      |       427 |
|       185 | MICHAEL     | BOLGER      |       761 |
|        37 | VAL         | BOLGER      |       663 |
|        37 | VAL         | BOLGER      |       997 |
|       129 | DARYL       | CRAWFORD    |       101 |
+-----------+-------------+-------------+-----------+
```

```
+-----------+---------------------+
| film_id   | title               |
+-----------+---------------------+
|       742 | ROOF CHAMPION       |
|       997 | YOUTH KICK          |
|       427 | HOMEWARD CIDER      |
|       761 | SANTA PARIS         |
|       663 | PATIENT SISTER      |
|       101 | BROTHERHOOD BLANKET |
+-----------+---------------------+
```

Each movie title is now accessible by its own key and none of them depends on non-film related information. Using the `film_id` column as a foreign key between the tables maintains the original connection the records had. Additionally, we've eliminated some redundancy by moving the movie titles to a new table. There's no wasted space from storing a movie title more than once.

The new table certainly follows 2NF, but we haven't entirely fixed the original table. We still have the same problem with actor names as we did with the film titles: not all of the columns that make up our key are logically related to the column whose value we want to target. This will be resolved when we apply the rules of 3NF. Normalization is a process and it's common for one form to serve as a stepping stone to the next, and for a form to satisfy more than just its own requirements.

Third Normal Form

A table is in Third Normal Form when the criteria for 2NF are met and all non-key fields are accessible by the table's primary key. We know we still have a problem with actor names because we can only target specific first_name and last_name fields by referencing actor_id and film_id. An actor's name doesn't depend on the films they starred in. actor_id is related logically to the names, but the duplication of values from following 1NF prohibits us from using it that way. We need to migrate the name columns to a separate table just as we did with the movie titles.

```
+----------+---------+
| actor_id | film_id |
+----------+---------+
|      124 |     742 |
|      124 |     997 |
|      185 |     427 |
|      185 |     761 |
|       37 |     663 |
|       37 |     997 |
|      129 |     101 |
+----------+---------+


+----------+------------+-----------+
| actor_id | first_name | last_name |
+----------+------------+-----------+
|      124 | SCARLETT   | BENING    |
|      185 | MICHAEL    | BOLGER    |
|       37 | VAL        | BOLGER    |
|      129 | DARYL      | CRAWFORD  |
+----------+------------+-----------+


+----------+---------------------+
```

```
| film_id | title                |
+---------+----------------------+
|     742 | ROOF CHAMPION        |
|     997 | YOUTH KICK           |
|     427 | HOMEWARD CIDER       |
|     761 | SANTA PARIS          |
|     663 | PATIENT SISTER       |
|     101 | BROTHERHOOD BLANKET  |
+---------+----------------------+
```

Moving the actor names to their own table permits us to use `actor_id` as the primary key for accessing them and again eliminates the duplication of data. What's left of our original table are the two ID columns which preserves the appearance connections. The result is not only 2NF, but also meets the requirements for 3NF.

The process of normalizing the table resulted in something that looks very similar to how the `sakila` database's `actor`, `film_actor`, and `film` tables are organized. Every column in the `actor` table has some logical connection to actors, each column in the `film` table pertains to movies, and the `film_actor` table is a junction table of foreign keys that maintain the relationships. A statement can join all three tables to identify the actors and their appearances, but the specific pieces of data are better organized and isolated from one another. Keeping 3NF in mind when planning out your tables goes a long way towards a well-designed database.

```
SELECT
    a.actor_id, a.first_name, a.last_name, f.film_id, f.title
FROM
    film_actor fa
    JOIN actor a ON fa.actor_id = a.actor_id
    JOIN film f ON fa.film_id = f.film_id;
```

Altering Tables

You may need to change the definition of an existing table when you normalizing an existing database, which is done using the `ALTER TABLE` statement. It lets us rename tables, add, remove, and rename columns, change column data types, add and delete keys and indexes, and even switch storage engines. To give you a taste of what `ALTER TABLE` statements look like, I'll show you a few that create and remove columns and indexes, since these are the most common actions needed for normalization.

An ALTER TABLE statement that adds a new column to a table looks like this:

```
ALTER TABLE actor ADD COLUMN bio VARCHAR(255) AFTER last_name;
```

The statement adds a `bio` column to the `actor` table to hold additional information about an actor. The definition for the column—in this case just a VARCHAR data type—is the same as what we would use in a CREATE TABLE. This means we can also specify attributes like a default value or NOT NULL if we want to. The position clause AFTER last_name instructs MySQL to place the new column after the last_name column in the table's definition. Without the clause, the column will be appended as the last column of the table.

Default Values

Each row will have its field for a newly created column set to the column's default value. If no default value is defined, the fields will be set to NULL.

An ALTER TABLE statement to delete the `bio` column looks like this:

```
ALTER TABLE actor DROP COLUMN bio;
```

To create an index, the ALTER TABLE statement looks like this:

```
ALTER TABLE actor ADD INDEX idx_last_update (last_update);
```

The statement creates an index named `idx_last_update` against the `last_update` column of the `actor` table. As with column definitions, the syntax to specify an index mirrors that used in the CREATE TABLE statement.

And here's the ALTER TABLE statement to drop the index:

```
ALTER TABLE actor DROP INDEX idx_last_update;
```

ALTER TABLE requires the index's name to drop it. If you don't know what its name is, either because you didn't provide an explicit name when you created it or because you simply forgot what you named it, you can find out by issuing a SHOW CREATE TABLE statement. Alternatively, you can send a SHOW INDEX statement:

```
SHOW INDEX FROM actor;
```

It's worth knowing that the `ALTER TABLE` statement allows us to provide multiple actions in the same statement. To provide more than one action, simply separate the actions with a comma, like so:

```
ALTER TABLE actor
    ADD COLUMN bio VARCHAR(255) AFTER last_name,
    ADD INDEX idx_last_update (last_update);
```

Conclusion

In this chapter, we've covered a lot information about working with multiple tables. You learned how to join tables in a `SELECT` statement, and also how to hide the complexity of such statements using views. We went through an exercise in normalization to see how 1NF, 2NF, and 3NF help us organize our database properly. And finally, I introduced you to `ALTER TABLE`, the statement used to modify the definition of an existing table.

As always, I encourage you to experiment with different scenarios to reinforce what you've learned here. Try to find the customers that rented the most movies. Are there customers whose rental habits show they have a favorite actor? Look through the other tables defined in the `sakila` database and observe how they follow 3NF.

It's also a good idea to search for additional resources that expand on the topics I've introduced. You can learn more about joins[4], views[5], and `ALTER TABLE`[6] in the documentation. Also, Wikipedia has a great write-up on normalization[7].

Now we'll look at MySQL from the programmer's perspective. In Chapter 5, we'll take a step back from SQL and see what communicating with MySQL looks like using Python, PHP, and R. Then, in Chapter 6, we'll see what facilities are available for programming MySQL and the database itself.

---

[4] http://dev.mysql.com/doc/refman/5.6/en/join.html

[5] http://dev.mysql.com/doc/refman/5.6/en/create-view.html

[6] http://dev.mysql.com/doc/refman/5.6/en/alter-table.html

[7] http://en.wikipedia.org/wiki/Database_normalization

Connecting from Code

It's more common for users to work with data stored in a database through an application's display than to directly send queries to the server using a command-line client. Although any specific details depend on the nature and purpose of each application, generally speaking the program provides an interface to accept input and display data, and some internal process to formulate queries and communicate with the database management system. Users may not even be aware their data is stored in a database behind all of that. In this chapter, we'll discuss the basics of communicating with MySQL from programming code.

There are many programming languages to choose from—even if we restrict ourselves to the most popular ones. Luckily, the popularity of MySQL pretty much guarantees that a library exists to connect to the server in whatever language you prefer. I've chosen to present three languages in this chapter: Python, because of its widespread use as a general-purpose programming language; PHP, because of its popularity with those who develop web-based applications; and R, because of its fast-growing use in statistics and data analysis.

Connecting from Python with Connector/Python

Python is the popular, dynamically-typed programming language created by Guido van Rossum. Since its first release in 1991, Python has found itself a home in scientific computing, information security, and general systems programming. Various desktop applications, such as LightWave 3D, GIMP, and LibreOffice, integrate Python to extend their capabilities through scripting. It was listed twice in TIOBE Software's Programming Language Hall of Fame (in 2007 and 2010), and has held a position in the top 10 of the TIOBE Programming Community Index since 2004.

There are several libraries available for working with MySQL in Python, of which the more popular are Connector/Python from Oracle, MySQLdb, and SQLAlchemy. We'll discuss Connector/Python here.

One of Connector/Python's most important features is that it implements MySQL's communication protocols completely in Python. For us, this means that no compilation or extra libraries are needed outside of the Python language itself. Connector/Python also conforms to PEP 249 (Python Database API Specification v2.0[1]) so what you learn from using this library is directly applicable to other libraries that conform to the same standard.

Connector/Python is available from various sources. The library is available for download from the MySQL website as a DEB package, RPM package, or MSI installer, and its source code was recently released on GitHub[2]. The library may even be available through your distro's package manager (Debian/Ubuntu users can run `sudo apt-get install python-mysql.connector`). But my personal preference for installing Python libraries is to use pip, so that's what I'll show here. To install Connector/Python with pip, open a terminal and execute the following command:

```
pip install --allow-external mysql-connector-python \
  mysql-connector-python
```

Connector/Python is hosted externally from pip's primary index which is why we need to provide the option `--allow-external` in the command above. The first in-

---

[1] https://www.python.org/dev/peps/pep-0249/
[2] http://github.com/oracle/mysql-connector-python

stance of `mysql-connector-python` is that option's argument, and the second is the requirement we want to install.

Basic Querying

Here's an example that shows what using Connector/Python—or any PEP 249-compliant database library for that matter—looks like:

```python
#! /usr/bin/env python

# Step 1: import the connector
import mysql.connector

# Step 2: open a connection
conn = mysql.connector.Connect(host="localhost", user="jump",
    password="secret", database="sakila")

# Step 3: obtain a cursor
cursor = conn.cursor()

# Step 4: construct and send a query
query = ("SELECT last_name, first_name FROM actor "
    "ORDER BY last_name, first_name")
cursor.execute(query)

# Step 5: iterate the results
for row in cursor:
    print("{:<45} {:<45}".format(*row))

# Step 6: clean up
cursor.close()
conn.close()
```

The `mysql.connector.Connect()` method accepts keyword arguments for the information necessary to establish a connection to MySQL and returns a `MySQLConnection` object. This object represents the connection between us and the server, and is used to commit/rollback transactions and obtain new instances of a `MySQLCursor` object. The term **cursor** refers to an internal structure used to iteratively process the rows in a result set. In general, you can think of the `MySQLCursor` object as an iterator that traverses a collection of records, one row at a time, making each available to us as a tuple.

Working with Positional Values

Elements in the result tuple are positionally defined by the order in which the column names appear in the SELECT statement. Working with positional values requires vigilance because it can be difficult to keep track of a large number of columns. Version 2 of Connector/Python will address this by introducing dictionary and named tuple results, but this is an enhancement not specified by PEP 249.

Besides iterating over the MySQLCursor object directly, we can use the fetchone(), fetchmany(), and fetchall() methods it offers, which do pretty much what each of their names imply. fetchone() returns the current row from the result, fetchmany() accepts an integer argument and returns a list of that many rows, and fetchall() returns a list containing all of the rows in the result set.

Here's an example that demonstrates the use of these cursor methods:

```python
# Just a convenience function for formatted output
def display(*row):
    print("{:<45} {:<45}".format(*row))

# send a query
query = ("SELECT last_name, first_name FROM actor "
    "ORDER BY last_name, first_name")
cursor.execute(query)

# fetch one row
row = cursor.fetchone()
display(*row)

# fetch the next 20 rows
rows = cursor.fetchmany(20)
for row in rows:
    display(*row)

# fetch all of the remaining rows
rows = cursor.fetchall()
for row in rows:
    display(*row)
```

Connector/Python disables autocommit by default, so statements that affect the database will not be committed automatically. This may take the uninitiated by surprise, and lead to head scratching when updates don't seem to stick. If you're using a transactional storage engine like InnoDB, it's necessary to commit your changes with the connection's commit() method. Statements in the transaction can alternatively be rolled back using the connection's rollback() method.

```
# send a query - affects the database
query = ("INSERT INTO actor (last_name, first_name) "
    "VALUES ('OLIVER', 'BRENDA')")
cursor.execute(query)

# commit the transaction
conn.commit()
```

Buffered and Unbuffered Results

The default behavior for Connector/Python is to use **unbuffered results**. This means that, whenever we issue a statement that returns data, all of the rows in the result set must be processed or an InternalError exception will be raised with the message "Unread results found." An unbuffered result set resides on the MySQL server, and each row is transmitted to the client when it's needed. **Buffered results**, on the other hand, are transferred immediately from MySQL and sit client-side where they wait to be accessed by our program. In a perfect world, we'd select only the data we intend to consume, but when the cursor will be closed prematurely, the way to avoid raising the exception is to use buffered results.

The MySQLCursorBuffered object is designed to buffer results. Whether we obtain a MySQLCursor or MySQLCursorBuffered instance from cursor() is determined by the argument buffered=True. We can pass the argument to connect() when we first open the connection to MySQL, and subsequent cursors created from it will be MySQLCursorBuffered objects. Alternatively, we can pass buffered=True to cursor() to obtain a MySQLCursorBuffered instance.

```
dbcreds = {
    "host": "localhost",
    "user": "jump",
    "password": "secret",
    "database": "sakila"
}

# connect to the database server. cursor() returns a MySQLCursor
# object
```

```
conn = mysql.connector.Connect(**dbcreds)
cursor = conn.cursor()
print(type(cursor))

# a second connection to the server. cursor() returns a
# MySQLBuffered object
conn2 = mysql.connector.Connect(buffered=True, **dbcreds)
cursor2 = conn2.cursor()
print(type(cursor2))

# cursor() returns a MySQLBuffered object
cursor3 = conn.cursor(buffered=True)
print(type(cursor3))
```

Prepared Statements

Sometimes the same basic statement is executed multiple times, but with different values each time. **Prepared statements** are often the most efficient route to take because the overhead for the server to parse and analyzing the statement is incurred only once. You can think of prepared statements as like a template: it provides a statement's syntax and column names, but placeholders appear where the data values would be. MySQL parses the template, but delays execution of the statement until it receives the missing values.

PEP 249 defines the following styles for specifying placeholders, but also states that libraries only need to implement one of them to be considered compliant:

■ Question mark — `WHERE first_name = ? AND last_name = ?`

■ Numeric position — `WHERE first_name = :1 AND last_name = :2`

■ Named parameter — `WHERE first_name = :fname AND last_name = :lname`

■ C-style format code — `WHERE first_name = %s AND last_name = %s`

■ Pyformat code — `WHERE first_name = %(fname)s AND last_name = %(lname)s`

Connector/Python supports the use of question marks and C-style format codes.

Placeholder Substitution

Connector/Python allows placeholder substitution for non-prepared statements (regular query statements) as well, although the placeholder styles are different. C-style format codes and Pyformat codes can be used for non-prepared statements. When C-style formatting is used, data values are passed as a tuple, along with the statement, to the cursor's `execute()` method. Values are passed as a dictionary to `execute()` when Pyformat codes are used.

The first step to using prepared statements is to instantiate a cursor object capable of handling them. This is done by passing the argument `prepared=True` to the connection object's `cursor()` method. The method then returns an instance of `MySQLCursorPrepared` which is a child class of `MySQLCursor`. The first time we call `execute()`, the cursor prepares the statement and executes it. Both the cursor and MySQL remember the statement for the duration of the connection and the prepare process is skipped for subsequent calls with the same statement.

```
# obtain a cursor capable of using prepared statements
cursor = conn.cursor(prepared=True)

# construct a query template (C-style format)
query = ("INSERT INTO actor (last_name, first_name) "
    "VALUES (%s, %s)")

# here's some data ...
records = [
    ("AFFLECK", "LAUREN"),
    ("BUTTERFIELD", "MIKE"),
    ("EASTERBROOK", "ANGELA")
]

# execute a query for each record
for row in records:
    cursor.execute(query, row)

# commit the transaction
conn.commit()
```

Because they handle data separately from the query statement, an additional benefit of using prepared statements is the protection they provide against SQL injection attacks. This is why many programmers prefer prepared statements—regardless of the number of times a statement is executed—when working with user-supplied data.

Connecting from PHP with PDO

PHP was released in 1995 by Rasmus Lerdof and quickly became the most popular server-side scripting language for developing dynamic websites and web-based applications. In large part, this was thanks to its gentle learning curve and integration into the web stack. PHP powers platforms such as MediaWiki and WordPress, and sites like Wikipedia, Facebook, and Etsy.

PHP also gained a reputation for being a sloppy language and a security risk; but while this was true in its early days, it certainly isn't true today. Efforts to clean up the language have restricted or removed features that were prone to abuse or attack, and modern-day PHP professionals are perhaps more conscious of security issues and best practices than their counterparts.

Two extensions are available for communicating with MySQL from PHP: the MySQLi extension, and the PDO extension. Here we'll take a look at PDO.

The MySQL Extension

A third extension, the MySQL extension, is deprecated and and will be moved to the PECL repository in PHP7. You may come across code that relies on it, simply because of the large amount of legacy PHP code still in production, but any new code you write should use either PDO or MySQLi.

PDO is made up of two parts: there's a high-level API that exposes objects to issue statements and iterate the results, and there are low-level drivers that handle resource management and the actual communication between PHP and the MySQL database server. This architecture has allowed PDO to consolidate a lot of functionality that was previously spread across different database extensions, such as MySQL, PostgreSQL, SQLite, and MSSQL. A programmer can now use the same API regardless of the server they work with.

PDO is part of the default PHP installation, but the MySQL driver needs to be installed separately. Debian/Ubuntu users can install it by running `sudo apt-get install php5-mysql`, and Red Hat/CentOS users can run `su -c 'yum install php-mysql'`. On Windows, all of the PDO drivers are included in the PHP installation's ext folder. You just need to update your php.ini file by adding or uncommenting the following line:

```
extension=php_pdo_mysql.dll
```

Basic Querying

Using PDO to interface with MySQL from PHP looks like this:

```php
<?php
// Step 1: open a connection
$db = new PDO("mysql:host=localhost;dbname=sakila", "jump",
    "secret");

// Step 2: construct and send a query
$query = "SELECT last_name, first_name FROM actor " .
    "ORDER BY last_name, first_name";
$result = $db->query($query);

// Step 3: iterate the results
echo "<ul>";
while ($row = $result->fetch()) {
    vprintf("<li>%s %s</li>", $row);
}
echo "</ul>";

// Step 4: clean up
$result->closeCursor();
$db = null;
```

Connecting to MySQL and selecting a database happens when we instantiate a new PDO object, passing to it a DSN string, username, and password. The term **DSN** is an abbreviation for Data Source Name, a string that identifies what low-level PDO driver should be used and any additional connection details that may be necessary.

The query() method returns an object instance of the PDOStatement class which offers several methods to retrieve rows from the query's result set: fetch(), fetchObject() and fetchAll(). The fetch() method returns rows one at a time, and fetchAll() returns an array of all of the orws. We can pass both methods a constant to specify how rows should be returned. The most common fetch styles are:

- PDO::FETCH_ASSOC — returns the row as an associative array with column names as the array keys

- PDO::FETCH_NUM — returns the row as an array with column positions as the array indexes

- PDO::FETCH_BOTH — returns the row as an array with members accessible by both column name and position (default behavior)

- PDO::FETCH_OBJECT — return the row as an anonymous object with column names as its public properties

The following example shows how each of these styles affects how we access the result's rows. You can visit the documentation for fetch()[3] to learn what other styles are available.

```
// just a convenience function for output
function display($lastName, $firstName) {
    echo "<div>{$lastName} {$firstName}</div>";
}

// send a query
$query = "SELECT last_name, first_name FROM actor " .
    "ORDER BY last_name, first_name";
$result = $db->query($query);

// fetch one row as associative array
$row = $result->fetch(PDO::FETCH_ASSOC);
display($row["last_name"], $row["first_name"]);

// fetch next row as numerically-indexed array
$rows = $result->fetch(PDO::FETCH_NUM);
display($row[0], $row[1]);

// fetch another row accessible both ways
$rows = $result->fetch(PDO::FETCH_BOTH);
display($row[0], $row[1]);
display($row["last_name"], $row["first_name"]);

// fetch all remaining rows as objects
```

---

[3] http://php.net/pdostatement.fetch

```
while ($row = $result->fetch(PDO::FETCH_OBJ)) {
    display($row->last_name, $row->first_name);
}
```

The fetchObject() method can be called without arguments, in which case it behaves pretty much like fetch(PDO::FETCH_OBJECT), but it's preferred that you provide the name of a class and possibly an array of constructor arguments with fetchObject(). The method creates an instance of the specified class, populates its properties with the record's details, and then invokes the constructor with any constructor arguments you provided. This example shows how to use fetchObject() to initialize an object with a result row:

```
// define a simple class
class Actor
{
    // properties initialized by PDO
    private $last_name;
    private $first_name;

    public function getLastName() {
        return $this->last_name;
    }
    public function getFirstName() {
        return $this->first_name;
    }
}

// send a query
$query = "SELECT last_name, first_name FROM actor " .
    "ORDER BY last_name, first_name";
$result = $db->query($query);

// instanciate an Actor object populated by query results
$row = $result->fetchObject("Actor");
display($row->getLastName(), $row->getFirstName());
```

 ### Understand How fetchObject() Behaves

It can be argued that fetchObject() is intrinsically broken because the method invokes the object's constructor after setting its properties. Property values set by the record can be overwritten by any initialization that takes place in the constructor. Before you use it, make sure you understand how `fetchObject()` behaves and whether it will play nice with your classes' constructors.

PDO uses buffered results by default, so all of the rows are sent immediately from MySQL and sit client-side where they wait to be accessed by PHP. Alternatively, unbuffered results only transmit a row from the MySQL server when it's needed. You can specify whether PDO should use buffered or unbuffered results by setting the `PDO::MYSQL_ATTR_USE_BUFFERED_QUERY` attribute like so:

```php
<?php
$db = new PDO("mysql:host=localhost;dbname=sakila", "jump",
    "secret");
// use buffered results, set false for unbuffered
$db->setAttribute(PDO::MYSQL_ATTR_USE_BUFFERED_QUERY, true);
```

When using unbuffered results, you must consume all of the rows or free the cursor's resources with `PDO::closeCursor()`. Otherwise, if you still have unread rows from a `SELECT` statement then any subsequent `INSERT` or `UPDATE` statements will silently fail. I suggest making a habit of using `closeCursor()` regardless, as I did in our first PHP example, to avoid such potentially frustrating situations.

Handling Errors

PDO can be configured in different ways to handle any errors it encounters when working with MySQL; we only need to pass the constant that represents the desired behavior to the `PDO` object's `setAttribute()` method. The error mode constants are:

- `PDO::ERRMODE_SILENT` — silent mode, does not interrupt the script's execution (default behavior)

- `PDO::ERRMODE_WARNING` — warning mode, triggers an `E_WARNING` message

- `PDO::ERRMODE_EXCEPTION` — exception mode, throws a `PDOException` object

No matter which behavior is configured, PDO internally stores information about any error it encounters. We can check the error using the `errorInfo()` method, which returns an array containing the five-character error string (defined by the ANSI SQL-92 standard), a driver-specific error code, and a driver-specific error message.

```
// Set error mode to silent
$db->setAttribute(PDO::ATTR_ERRMODE, PDO::ERRMODE_SILENT);

// submit a malformed query
$query = "MALFORMED QUERY";
$result = $db->query($query);

// display the error details
print_r($db->errorInfo());
```

When we specify exception mode, the description of what went wrong is available with the exception object's getMessage() method.

```
// set error mode to exception
$db->setAttribute(PDO::ATTR_ERRMODE, PDO::ERRMODE_EXCEPTION);

// submit a malformed query
$query = "MALFORMED QUERY";
try {
    $result = $db->query($query);
}
catch (PDOException $e) {
    // Display the exception message
    echo $e->getMessage();
}
```

Prepared Statements

As I mentioned earlier with Connector/Python, prepared statements are primarily an efficient way to execute the same statement multiple times, but they also implicitly guard against injection attacks because data is handled separately from the statement. PHP is used mainly for developing back ends for web-based applications and dynamic sites, and injection attacks are one of the most common security vulnerabilities faced by such platforms. It should come as no surprise then that most PHP programmers take advantage of the secondary benefit of prepared statements—that of protecting against injection attacks—and use them exclusively.

To use prepared statements, we first provide the statement template to the PDO object's prepare() method with placeholders appearing where the data values would be. PDO supports both anonymous positional placeholders (?) and named placeholders (:name). We then send the partial statement to the server and are returned a `PDOStatement` object instance. We pass the data values to the object's `execute()` method to execute the statement.

```
// construct a query template
$query = "INSERT INTO actor (last_name, first_name) VALUES " .
    "(:last, :first)";

// prepare the statement
$stmt = $db->prepare($query);

// here's some data...
$records = [
    ["last" => "AFFLECK", "first" => "LAUREN"],
    ["last" => "BUTTERFIELD", "first" => "MIKE"],
    ["last" => "EASTERBROOK", "first" => "ANGELA"]
];

// execute the query for each record
foreach ($records as $row) {
    $stmt->execute($row);
}
```

Connecting from R with RMySQL

Created by Robert Gentleman and Ross Ihaka in 1996, R is a modern implementation of the S programming language and is a feature-rich programming environment specifically tailored for data analysis and visualization. R's popularity has grown rapidly among data miners and scientists, surpassing the use of Excel, Python, and SAS for such work. Companies like Facebook, Google, ANZ Bank, and Pfizer have all used R to gain better insight into their research data.

Although an R programmer may be more accustomed to consuming data for analysis from Excel spreadsheets or CSV files than from a database servers, working with such servers can be useful when data is shared between many applications, or when full calculations would exhaust R's available memory. Performing operations in MySQL before the records are retrieved can make working in R easier, too. For example, computing quantiles on sorted data is much easier. From MySQL's perspective, R is also a nice complement with its graphing capabilities and comprehensive statistics and data analysis functionality.

The library scene for working with MySQL is not as diverse for R as it is for the other languages we've discussed. The DBI package provides virtual classes that establish a common interface for working with relational database systems, and other packages extend DBI to work with their target database. As MySQL users, we'll be looking at the RMySQL library.

If you're using a Linux distro, RMySQL may be available through your system's package manager (Ubuntu users can install it with the command `apt-get install r-cran-mysql`). RMySQL is also available in CRAN, the Comprehensive R Archive Network, so we can just as easily install the package from within the R environment itself. When it's installed in this manner, the source code for RMySQL will be downloaded to your system and compiled locally, so you'll need a suitable compiler tool chain, and have the MySQL client library and header files installed.

Executing the following code within R will download, compile, and install RMySQL from the indicated CRAN repository. DBI will also be installed automatically if it hasn't been installed already:

```
install.packages("RMySQL", repos="http://cran.rstudio.com")
```

 Installation Issues

Troubleshooting anything that goes wrong in the compilation process is beyond the scope of this book. There are many online resources you can turn to if you encounter an issue. A good starting point is to search for any distinct error messages you encounter using your favorite search engine.

Working with Tables

Using the `dbReadTable()` method, we can conveniently read the contents of an entire table into an R dataframe. However, you should check whether the data can fit comfortably in R's available memory. This goes beyond just pushing table rows into memory; it also involves minding the amount that's consumed at various points in your analysis.

Using RMySQL to import the entire table from MySQL into an R dataframe looks like this:

```
#! /usr/bin/env Rscript

# Step 1: import library
library(RMySQL)

# Step 2: open a connection
con <- dbConnect(MySQL(), user="jump", password="secret",
                 host="localhost", dbname="sakila")

# Step 3: read the table into a dataframe
dframe <- dbReadTable(con, "actor")

# Step 4: analyze the data
summary(dframe)

# Step 5: cleanup
dbDisconnect(con)
rm(con)
```

The dbConnect() method connects to the MySQL server and returns a MySQLConnection object that represents the connection between us and the server. The first argument is mandatory—a DBIDriver object—which I created and passed inline using MySQL(). In this case, RMySQL behaves like PHP's PDO extension, in that it separates the implementation of the DBI classes from the lower-level driver logic. The remaining arguments are the authentication parameters needed to successfully connect to the MySQL server.

dbReadTable() then receives the connection object and the name of the table we want to import. It retrieves the entire contents of the table and returns it as a dataframe. The mapping between MySQL's datatypes and R's Integer, Numeric, and Character types is a bit imperfect (the RMySQL driver's source code is full of comments that reflect the developer's frustration in this regard). Observe any warnings that might be issued, and ensure any type coercion or casting doesn't jeopardize the integrity of your results.

Finally, the dbDisconnect() method closes the connection and frees any resources.

It's also possible to go the other way and create a table in the database from the contents of a dataframe using the dbWriteTable() method. This method takes at minimum the connection object, a name for the table that will be created, and a dataframe of rows to populate the table. This is a convenient way to push the intermediate data of an analysis, or its results, to a database where it can be made available to other applications. Don't count on the resulting column definitions to be very precise, though. Columns created with dbWriteTable() will be typed mostly as TEXT or DOUBLE. You'll need to issue an ALTER TABLE statement separately if you want to change any of the definitions or add any indexes.

```
# create a duplicate actor table without row_names column
dbWriteTable(con, "actor_dupe", dframe)
```

RMySQL also adds a TEXT column named row_names to the new table which stores the name from the dataframe that the record had. If the rows already have a column suitable for use as a primary key, this column is redundant. We can suppress it by passing the argument row.names=FALSE.

```
# create a duplicate actor table without row_names column
dbWriteTable(con, "actor_dupe", dframe, row.names=FALSE)
```

Basic Querying

Given the nature of work typically done in R, it's safe to say it's more common to import and export data using dbReadTable() and dbWriteTable() than to issue a query statement and iteratively process the results. But when we do need such query/result functionality—for example, if we want to sort the rows before bringing them into R—we can use dbGetQuery() and dbSendQuery().

The dbGetQuery() method accepts the connection object and an SQL statement. It then executes the statement and returns a dataframe populated with all of the result's rows. Here's an example:

```
query <- paste0("SELECT last_name, first_name FROM actor ",
                "ORDER BY last_name, first_name")
dframe <- dbGetQuery(con, query)
```

To retrieve the rows iteratively, either one by one or in chunks, we use the db-SendQuery(). Unlike dbGetQuery() query, this method executes the statement but doesn't return any rows. Instead, it returns a MySQLResult object which we use with the dbFetch() and dbHasCompleted() methods to read in the result's rows.

```
query <- paste0("SELECT last_name, first_name FROM actor ",
                "ORDER BY last_name, first_name")
res <- dbSendQuery(con, query)
while (!dbHasCompleted(res)) {
  # retrieve data 20 rows at a time
  chunk <- dbFetch(res, n=20)
  # do something with the data
  print(chunk)
}
# free the result set
dbClearResult(res)
```

Before each iteration of the while loop, the dbHasCompleted() method inspects the state of the resource and returns whether or not all rows have been retrieved. The n argument to dbFetch() instructs the method to return a dataframe of up that many rows of data (I retrieved 20 rows in the example above). If we give n=-1, dbFetch() will return a dataframe with all of the remaining rows. RMySQL results are unbuffered, so it's important to make sure all of them are consumed and any used resources are freed using dbClearResult().

Conclusion

You now know what working with MySQL looks like from the programmer's perspective. The approach to interfacing with MySQL is generally consistent across languages and libraries: establish a connection, send a statement, receive the results, and terminate the connection. The finer details of reading in records is what differs—for example, whether the result set is buffered or unbuffered and how values are converted between MySQL's type system and the programming language's.

I did my best to weigh popularity and purpose when selecting the languages and libraries to discuss here. I'm sorry if your preferred language/library wasn't among them, but don't panic! Consider this chapter helpful in understanding the general concepts of working with MySQL from code. Now that you understand the basics, you can more easily understand another language/library's resources.

The next chapter will give us a look at programming from MySQL's perspective. We'll see how to program MySQL with stored procedures and triggers, routines that execute within a MySQL database. We'll also see how to write custom functions to use in our statements, like COUNT() and SUM() are.

Chapter 6

Programming the Database

A **stored routine** is a set of statements stored and executed in the database. From the perspective of a database administrator, routines can provide an additional level of security because we can give users access through an API of routines instead of allowing them to access or modify data in the tables directly. From the programmer's perspective, routines can improve an application's performance in some cases because they process data while it's still in the database. The logic may execute more efficiently, because of things like server hardware and programming language choices, and aggregate calculations (such as summation, averaging, etc.) reduce the amount of data sent across the network back to an application. To help reduce code duplication, logic that's common to various applications using the same database can even be written as stored routines.

Stored routines in MySQL are written using a procedural language that closely adheres to SQL/PSM, a standard that extends SQL with common programming concepts like variables, IF constructs, and loops. SQL/PSM itself was inspired by Ada, a language created at the behest of the US Department of Defense in 1979 for programming embedded computer systems, and shares much of the same syntax.

In this chapter, we'll see what some of the basic constructs look like in SQL and then look at the four types of routines available: stored procedures, functions, triggers, and events. I'll also show you how to write user-defined functions in C and how to register them with MySQL, making them appear like a native, built-in function. Whereas Chapter 5 focused on programming *with* a database, this chapter is about programming *in* the database.

Learning the Basics

The body of a stored routine can consist of many statements, but MySQL expects us to provide its definition as a single statement. This is a problem when we're using the command-line client because the client isn't smart enough to distinguish the semicolons terminating the statements in the routine's body from the semicolon that terminates the defining statement itself. The solution is to change the current session's delimiter to something other than a semicolon. It can be reset to practically anything, but $$ or // are the most common choices, because they're not likely to appear in the definition.

The DELIMITER command to change the delimiter to $$ is:

```
DELIMITER $$
```

To change the delimiter back to the semicolon, the command is:

```
DELIMITER ;
```

 Resetting the Delimiter

Get in the habit of setting the delimiter back to a semicolon after you finish defining your routine. Otherwise, you'll inevitably type it by force of habit and the client will sit patiently waiting for the current delimiter. Aside from feeling a bit foolish, though, it's not a big deal if you forget. Typing the current delimiter after the inadvertent semicolon will submit the statement without issue. (And then you can change the delimiter!)

There are three kinds of variables you'll encounter when writing routines for MySQL, and each has a different form and scope from the others. They are:

- Local variables — the variable appears in the body of a routine and is named as a bare literal (for example, my_var). Local variables are scoped to a BEGIN/END block and defined using DECLARE. They are automatically initialized to NULL every time the routine is executed. Parameters in a procedure definition are also local variables.

- Session variables — the variable can appear pretty much anywhere, inside or outside of a routine. Session variable names carry the leading sigil @ (for example, @my_var) and are initialized to NULL. They behave similarly to global variables in programming languages like C, PHP, and Ruby, unconcerned with the scope they're used in. Session variables exist for the duration of the connection to the MySQL server.

- System variables — the variable is predefined by MySQL and is used to inspect or change the behavior of the server and connection environment. Global system variables affecting the MySQL server are either annotated with the keyword GLOBAL or carry the prefix @@global. (for example, GLOBAL time_format or @@global.time_format). Session system variables affecting the connection of individual clients are annotated with the keyword SESSION or are prefixed with @@session. (for example, SESSION time_zone or @@session.time_zone).

Assigning a value to a variable looks like this:

```
SET my_var = 42;
```

Variables can also be set from the results of a SELECT statement using INTO. The INTO keyword redirects the column values to the designated variables, so the number of columns and variables in the statement must match, and the result set can only contain one row.

```
SELECT first_name, last_name INTO @fname, @lname FROM
actor WHERE id = 7;
```

The ability to take a different course of action based on whether a given condition holds true is one of the staples of any programming language, so naturally IF is included among the procedural programming constructs that augment SQL. It behaves exactly as you would expect.

```
IF my_var >  0 THEN
    SELECT 'value is positive';
ELSEIF my_var < 0 THEN
    SELECT 'value is negative';
ELSE
    SELECT 'value is zero';
END IF;
```

The keyword IF begins the construct followed by a conditional expression, and THEN introduces the branch's body. Multiple branches are provided, each with their own conditions using ELSEIF, and ELSE marks the final default block. END IF marks the end of the entire construct.

Sometimes it's more convenient to organize logic into a CASE construct, especially when the conditions all test the same variable but for a different value. The CASE construct uses the keywords CASE and WHEN like this:

```
CASE rating
WHEN 'G', 'PG', 'PG-13' THEN
    SELECT 'family friendly';
WHEN 'R' THEN
    SELECT 'adults only';
ELSE
    SELECT 'unknown rating';
END CASE;
```

The same set of statements can be executed in a loop using flow control constructs like WHILE and REPEAT. MySQL's WHILE construct tests its condition at the beginning of each iteration, and repeatedly executes the body for as long as the condition holds true. The construct looks like this:

```
WHILE countdown > 0 DO
    SET countdown = countdown - 1;
END WHILE;
```

The REPEAT construct tests its condition at the end of an iteration and continues to loop over statements until the condition is true. In other words, it loops while the condition is false. The REPEAT construct looks like this:

```
REPEAT
    SET countdown = countdown - 1;
UNTIL countdown = 0
END REPEAT;
```

MySQL also offers cursors for programmatic iteration of a result set in a stored procedure. A local variable is defined in the procedure as CURSOR followed by a SELECT statement. The statement is executed and the cursor is initialized with OPEN. FETCH reads the current row's values into variables and advances the cursor to the next row. CLOSE frees the cursor. Also useful when working with cursors is the built-in FOUND_ROWS() function which returns the number of rows in the result set of the last SELECT statement executed.

```
DECLARE id, i INTEGER UNSIGNED;
DECLARE name CHAR(45);
DECLARE curs CURSOR FOR SELECT customer_id, last_name
  FROM customer;

OPEN curs;
SET i = FOUND_ROWS();
WHILE i > 0 THEN
    SET i = i - 1;
    FETCH curs INTO id, name;
END WHILE;
CLOSE curs;
```

Last but not least, there are several ways to provide comments in SQL code:

```
-- this is a single-line comment

# this is another single-line comment

/* this comment can span
   multiple lines */
```

Functions

A **function** is a stored routine that accepts input via arguments and returns a value to the calling context. Functions are used directly in expressions and statements, just like the native functions COUNT(), MAX(), and SUM() that we saw in earlier chapters.

Functions can be classified into two broad groups, based on their behavior: **aggregate functions**, and **singe-value functions**. All of the built-in functions we've seen are aggregate functions. Their logic is repeatedly executed over a set of inputs and the result is a single value reduced from all of the inputs. Single-value functions behave like the typical function or method in most programming languages with each input executing independently from any others. Custom aggregate functions must be written as UDFs using C or C++, so we'll discuss them later. Right now, we'll concern ourselves only with single-value functions.

Suppose we want to format the film titles for display with the first letter of each word capitalized and the remaining letters in lower case. MySQL offers a selection of string-related functions already, but unfortunately, none of them do exactly what we want to do here. We have two possible options. Either we can retrieve a title and format it in our application's code (assuming we're working with MySQL pro-grammatically) or write a stored routine to do the formatting, which we can then use directly in our SELECT statements. Since we're talking about programming MySQL, let's go the SQL route.

Here's how a CREATE FUNCTION statement defines the custom function:

```
DELIMITER $$

CREATE FUNCTION UCWords (
    string VARCHAR(255)
) RETURNS VARCHAR(255)
BEGIN
    DECLARE buffer VARCHAR(255) DEFAULT '';
    DECLARE word   VARCHAR(255);
    DECLARE pos    TINYINT UNSIGNED;

    REPEAT
        -- pop word from beginning of string
        SET pos = LOCATE(' ', string);
        IF pos > 0 THEN
            SET word = SUBSTRING(string, 1, pos - 1);
            SET string = SUBSTRING(string, pos + 1);
        ELSE
            -- reached the last word
            SET word = string;
            SET string = '';
        END IF;
```

```
        SET word = CONCAT(
            UPPER(SUBSTRING(word, 1, 1)),
            LOWER(SUBSTRING(word, 2)));

        SET buffer = CONCAT(buffer, ' ', word);
    UNTIL LENGTH(string) = 0
    END REPEAT;

    -- trim leading space
    RETURN SUBSTRING(buffer, 2);
END$$

DELIMITER ;
```

The CREATE FUNCTION statement creates a custom, single-value function named
UCWords(). The function accepts a VARCHAR argument as input (the film title) and
returns the formatted string (also a VARCHAR). The execution of the function stops
when the RETURN statement is encountered, and the value of the RETURN expression
is sent directly back to the calling environment. When the body contains more than
one statement, the statements must be grouped in a BEGIN/END block. This is optional
when the body contains only a single statement, though I like to provide BEGIN/END
regardless for the sake of consistency.

 Built-in String Functions

Several built-in string functions are used in the body of UCWords to slice, dice,
and transform the input. A list of available functions can be found in the documentation[1].

The stored function can be used just like any native function in an expression or
statement.

```
SELECT UCWords(title) AS title FROM film ORDER BY title;
+--------------------------------+
| UCWords(title)                 |
+--------------------------------+
| Academy Dinosaur               |
| Ace Goldfinger                 |
```

---

[1] http://dev.mysql.com/doc/refman/5.6/en/functions.html

```
| Adaptation Holes           |
⋮
| Zoolander Fiction          |
| Zorro Ark                  |
+----------------------------+
1000 rows in set (0.02 sec)
```

Stored functions can be convenient because they're easier to write than UDFs, but it's important to keep in mind that they also execute more slowly than their compiled counterparts. This is because they're interpreted by MySQL. This may prove problematic when called repeatedly in a statement that retrieves a large result set.

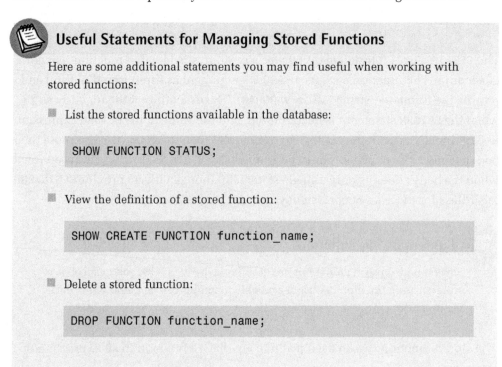

Useful Statements for Managing Stored Functions

Here are some additional statements you may find useful when working with stored functions:

- List the stored functions available in the database:

```
SHOW FUNCTION STATUS;
```

- View the definition of a stored function:

```
SHOW CREATE FUNCTION function_name;
```

- Delete a stored function:

```
DROP FUNCTION function_name;
```

Stored Procedures

Stored procedures are essentially small programs stored in the database. Whereas functions are used for calculations, procedures are intended for more general tasks or to execute business logic. They're invoked by a CALL statement with the procedure's name and possibly any parameters it takes. In addition to passing information to the procedure using parameters, we send values back out to the calling environment via the parameters as well.

Let's say we want a convenient way to generate a small report that lists how many outstanding rentals a customer has and what the movie titles are. As you might suspect, we can do this with a stored procedure. Here's an example of a CREATE PROCEDURE statement that defines a procedure named customer_rentals:

```
DELIMITER $$

CREATE PROCEDURE rental_report (
    IN cust_id INTEGER UNSIGNED,
    OUT film_count TINYINT
) BEGIN
    DECLARE cust_name VARCHAR(92);
    DECLARE i INTEGER;
    -- cursors must be declared after all other variables
    DECLARE curs CURSOR FOR SELECT
        UCWords(CONCAT(c.last_name, ', ', c.first_name)),
        COUNT(i.film_id)
    FROM
        rental r
        JOIN inventory i ON r.inventory_id = i.inventory_id
        JOIN customer c ON r.customer_id = c.customer_id
    WHERE
        r.return_date IS NULL
        AND r.customer_id = cust_id
    GROUP BY
        r.customer_id;

    OPEN curs;
    IF FOUND_ROWS() > 0 THEN
        FETCH curs INTO cust_name, film_count;

        -- header
        (SELECT
            cust_id AS `CUSTOMER ID`,
            cust_name AS `CUSTOMER NAME`,
            film_count AS `RENTALS`)
        UNION

        -- list film rentals
        (SELECT
            ' ', ' ', UCWords(f.title)
        FROM
            rental r
            JOIN inventory i ON r.inventory_id = i.inventory_id
```

```
                    JOIN film f ON i.film_id = f.film_id
            WHERE
                    r.return_date IS NULL
                    AND r.customer_id = cust_id
            ORDER BY
                    f.title);
        ELSE
            SET film_count = 0;
            SELECT
                customer_id AS `CUSTOMER ID`,
                UCWords(CONCAT(last_name, ', ', first_name))
                    AS `CUSTOMER NAME`,
                0 AS `RENTALS`
            FROM
                customer
            WHERE
                customer_id = cust_id;
        END IF;
        CLOSE curs;
    END$$

    DELIMITER ;
```

CREATE PROCEDURE gives a name for the procedure, a list of parameters, and any statements that make up the body of the routine. In particular, rental_report accepts a customer ID, outputs the desired report of the customer's outstanding rentals, and returns the number of rentals through its OUT parameter.

Calling the procedure looks like this:

```
CALL rental_report(560, @count);
+-------------+-------------------+-------------------+
| CUSTOMER ID | CUSTOMER NAME     | RENTALS           |
+-------------+-------------------+-------------------+
| 560         | Archuleta, Jordan | 2                 |
|             |                   | Pianist Outfield  |
|             |                   | Movie Shakespeare |
+-------------+-------------------+-------------------+
```

```
3 rows in set (0.00 sec)

Query OK, 0 rows affected (0.01 sec)
```

After invoking `rental_report`, the `@count` variable is populated and can be used in subsequent statements.

```
SELECT @count;
+---------+
| @count |
+---------+
|       2 |
+---------+
1 row in set (0.00 sec)
```

Useful Statements for Managing Stored Procedures

Here are some additional statements you may find useful when working with stored procedures:

■ List the stored procedures available in the database:

```
SHOW PROCEDURE STATUS;
```

■ View the definition of a stored procedure:

```
SHOW CREATE PROCEDURE procedure_name;
```

■ Delete a stored procedure:

```
DROP PROCEDURE procedure_name;
```

Triggers

A **trigger** is a stored routine that's automatically invoked by MySQL. Triggers are bound to a table and execute either before or after an `INSERT`, `UPDATE`, or `DELETE` statement is performed, depending on how we define them.

Suppose we want to know the average amount a customer spends so we can gauge the relationship they have with our stores and the clerk can potentially upsell any less profitable transactions. We can glean this information from the database ourselves, but we can also use some custom stored functions, and a trigger, to have MySQL calculate and maintain the information for us in real time.

First, add two new columns to the customer table to record the number of payments and the average amount for each customer.

```
ALTER TABLE customer
    ADD COLUMN payment_count INTEGER NOT NULL DEFAULT 0,
    ADD COLUMN average_amount DECIMAL(5,2) NOT NULL DEFAULT 0.00;
```

The new fields in each row are all initialized to 0, so next we need to populate them. Running a SELECT statement with COUNT()—to count the number of payment records in the payment table for a given customer—will give us the value for their record's payment_count. By issuing a SELECT statement that uses AVG(), a built-in aggregate function that returns the average of its set of inputs, we can find out what all of the customer's payments average out to. Each statement can be wrapped in a function that returns the desired value which we can then use in a simple UPDATE statement to fill in the values across the entire table instead of filling them in all manually.

```
DELIMITER $$

CREATE FUNCTION tally_payment_count (
    id SMALLINT UNSIGNED
) RETURNS INTEGER UNSIGNED
BEGIN
    DECLARE pay_count INTEGER UNSIGNED;

    SELECT COUNT(customer_id) INTO pay_count FROM payment WHERE
        customer_id = id;

    RETURN pay_count;
END $$

CREATE FUNCTION tally_average_amount (
    id SMALLINT UNSIGNED
) RETURNS DECIMAL(5,2)
BEGIN
    DECLARE avg_amnt DECIMAL(5,2);
```

```
    SELECT AVG(amount) INTO avg_amnt FROM payment WHERE
        customer_id = id;

    RETURN avg_amnt;
END $$

DELIMITER ;
```

We then fill the payment_count and average_amount fields by calling the functions in the following UPDATE statement:

```
UPDATE customer SET
    payment_count = tally_payment_count(customer_id),
    average_amount = tally_average_amount(customer_id);
```

Now we're faced with the problem of maintaining these columns going forward. If we were to run the UPDATE statement just periodically, the values in customer won't always be current. It's preferable to issue the update for a customer every time a payment is made, and performing this via a trigger bound to the payment table ensures that it will happen for every transaction without any manual effort.

```
DELIMITER $$

CREATE TRIGGER maintain_customer_spending_after_payment_insert
AFTER INSERT ON payment
FOR EACH ROW
BEGIN
    UPDATE customer SET
        payment_count = tally_payment_count(NEW.customer_id),
        average_amount = tally_average_amount(NEW.customer_id)
    WHERE
        customer_id = NEW.customer_id;
END $$

DELIMITER ;
```

Triggers can be invoked either before or after an action takes place. Here, AFTER INSERT specifies that maintain_customer_spending_after_payment_insert should execute after MySQL inserts the row into the payment table. If I specified BEFORE INSERT instead, MySQL would execute the trigger before it inserts the row. Only one trigger per time/action pairing can be assigned to a table. That is, you can define a trigger to execute before an update, and another to execute after the update, but you can't define two BEFORE UPDATE triggers for the same table.

Triggers don't accept input from parameters like the other stored routines we've seen. They do, however, have access to the row's modified values. For INSERT statements, the new values added to the table are accessible by prefixing NEW. to their column name, and the old values that are removed by a DELETE statement are available by prefixing OLD. to their column name. Since UPDATE statements replace existing values, OLD. provides access to the original values, and NEW. provides access to their replacements.

 Working Around Limitations

To work around the one trigger per time/action per table limitation, you can place your logic in various stored procedures and then use a trigger as the driving mechanism to call them. For example, you can't write something like this:

```
CREATE TRIGGER foo AFTER INSERT ON mytable …
CREATE TRIGGER bar AFTER INSERT ON mytable …
```

But you *can* write something like this:

```
CREATE PROCEDURE foo …
CREATE PROCEDURE bar …

CREATE TRIGGER mytable_after_insert
AFTER INSERT ON mytable FOR EACH ROW
BEGIN
    CALL foo();
    CALL bar();
END $$
```

 Useful Statements for Managing Triggers

Here are some additional statements you may find useful when working with triggers:

▪ List the definitions of all triggers:

```
SHOW TRIGGERS;
```

■ View the definition of a specific trigger:

```
SHOW TRIGGERS LIKE 'trigger_name';
```

■ Delete a trigger:

```
DROP TRIGGER procedure_name;
```

Events

Events are sometimes referred to as "temporal triggers" because they are routines scheduled to run at a certain time. They're similar in concept to the Unix scheduling services `cron` and `at`, or Windows Task Scheduler, except they live in the database. The advantage of events is that they're cross platform; since they run in the database, we're not tied to a specific platform scheduler.

MySQL has a dedicated event scheduler subsystem that's responsible for executing events at the correct time. The global system variable `event_scheduler` is used to turn the scheduler system on and off. By default, the scheduler isn't running, so we need to set `event_scheduler` to "ON" to start it.

```
SET GLOBAL event_scheduler = ON;
```

Events are defined/scheduled using `CREATE EVENT`. Here's an example that sets any rows in the `customer` table to inactive if the customer's data in the `rental` table shows they haven't rented a movie in the past three years:

```
DELIMITER $$

CREATE EVENT inactive_customer_maintenance
    ON SCHEDULE
        EVERY 1 DAY
    DO
BEGIN
```

```
    UPDATE
        customer c
        JOIN rental r ON c.customer_id = r.customer_id
    SET
        c.active = 0
    WHERE
        r.rental_date < DATE_SUB(NOW(), INTERVAL 3 YEAR);
END$$

DELIMITER ;
```

Following ON SCHEDULE, the keyword AT can be used to schedule a run-once event, followed by the timestamp of when the event should execute. For example, ON SCHEDULE AT '2015-11-03 00:00:00' registers the event to run at midnight on November 3rd. Alternatively, EVERY is used to specify a recurring interval. The example event above is scheduled to run once every day.

Events can be scheduled to execute just once or on a recurring basis. Recurring events can repeat indefinitely or for a specific duration. Although our example repeats forever, STARTS and ENDS can be used to bracket the time in which the event is valid. Start and end times can be specified as datetime values, or as relative values using intervals.

```
CREATE EVENT inactive_customer_maintenance
    ON SCHEDULE
        EVERY 1 DAY
        STARTS CURRENT_TIMESTAMP
        ENDS CURRENT_TIMESTAMP + INTERVAL 1 MONTH
    DO
BEGIN
...
```

Interval expressions are provided using the keyword INTERVAL followed by a unit and measure. For example, INTERVAL 1 MONTH for one month, and INTERVAL 5 HOUR for five hours. Available measures include YEAR, QUARTER, MONTH, WEEK, DAY, MINUTE, and SECOND. More complex measures are YEAR_MONTH, DAY_HOUR, DAY_MINUTE, DAY_SECOND, HOUR_MINUTE, HOUR_SECOND, and MINUTE_SECOND. When using these, the unit is a string with the two parts separated by a colon. INTERVAL '1:12' DAY_HOUR, for example, means every 1 day and 12 hours.

MySQL will automatically delete events after they've run through the duration of their schedule. We can add ON COMPLETION PRESERVE to the definition to preserve them, like so:

```
CREATE EVENT my_zombie_event
    ON SCHEDULE
        EVERY 1 DAY
        ENDS CURRENT_TIMESTAMP + INTERVAL 1 MONTH
        ON COMPLETION PRESERVE
    DO
BEGIN
...
```

 Useful Statements for Managing Events

Here are some additional statements you may find useful when working with events:

- List events and their status:

  ```
  SHOW EVENTS;
  ```

- View the definition of an event:

  ```
  SHOW CREATE EVENT event_name;
  ```

- Disable/enable an event:

  ```
  ALTER EVENT event_name DISABLE;
  ALTER EVENT event_name ENABLE;
  ```

- Delete an event:

  ```
  DROP EVENT event_name;
  ```

User-defined Functions

A **user-defined function** (UDF) is code written in C or C++ which is then compiled into a library and loaded into MySQL as a plugin. There are several reasons why we might want to do this: a function written in C is more performant than one written in SQL; such functions can access system libraries and expose functionality that otherwise wouldn't be available; and custom, aggregate-value functions must be written as UDFs because no other facility exists to cleanly maintain the accumulator for their final result.

 UDF Libraries

A small collection of UDF libraries is available at http://www.mysqludf.org and http://www.fromdual.com/mysql-plugins-and-udfs. You can also search public repositories on sites like GitHub to find useful functions.

Minimally, a UDF implementation consists of three C/C++ functions:

- *myfunc*_init() — initializes any resources needed by *myfunc*().

- *myfunc*() — performs the actual work of the function.

- *myfunc*_deinit() — frees any resources initialized by *myfunc*_init() and used in *myfunc*().

MySQL calls these functions when a user invokes the UDF in the manner illustrated in Figure 6.1.

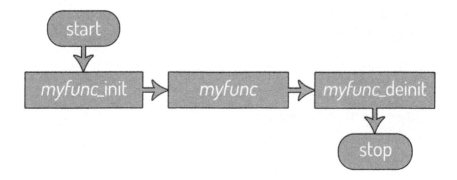

Figure 6.1. Calling order of the underlying functions when a single-value UDF is used.

Aggregate functions also implement *myfunc*_clear() to reset the accumulator before each set, and *myfunc*_add() to update the accumulator for each value. The calls in an aggregate-value UDF are illustrated in Figure 6.2.

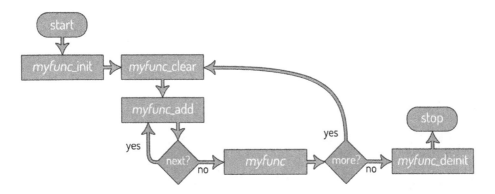

Figure 6.2. Calling order of the underlying functions when an aggregate-value UDF is used.

In each of the names, I've used *myfunc* as a placeholder. In the actual implementation, *myfunc* would be replaced with the name of UDF function as it would appear to the end user.

Let's walk through an aggregate-value function in C and create a UDF that returns an integer's Benford value based on a set of inputs. Benford's law states the distribution of the first digits in a set of numbers should follow a specific pattern. The digit 1, for example, should appear approximately 30% of the time as the leading digit, whereas the digit 9 should appear less than 5% of the time in that position. A number's Benford value is thus the percentage of its appearance as the first digit in all the values in the set.

Benford's Law

Benford's law has has been used to detect fraud in election results and accounting activities. You can read up on it on the Data Genetics blog[2] and see it in action at testingbenfordslaw.com[3].

First, there are the typical includes, function prototypes, and typedefs like you would see in any C code:

---

[2] http://datagenetics.com/blog/march52012/index.html

[3] http://testingbenfordslaw.com

```
#include <stdlib.h>
#include <string.h>
#include "mysql.h"

my_bool benford_init(UDF_INIT *, UDF_ARGS *, char *);
void benford_deinit(UDF_INIT *);
void benford_clear(UDF_INIT *, UDF_ARGS *, char *, char *);
void benford_add(UDF_INIT *, UDF_ARGS *, char *, char *);
double benford(UDF_INIT *, UDF_ARGS *, char *, char *, char *);

typedef struct
{
    int seen;   /* count of times the digit is seen */
    int rows;   /* the number of rows processed */
}
benford_data;
```

The `mysql.h` header defines the client API to work with MySQL. You should have it if you installed MySQL from source, but if you installed MySQL via a package manager, you'll probably need to install the development package for the mysqlclient library as well. On Ubuntu, the package is `libmysqlclient-dev`.

`UDF_INIT` is the main data structure passed between the functions by MySQL. It contains values that affect the behavior and return value of the UDF as well as a pointer we can assign to share our `bendford_data` struct. `UDF_ARGS` is a structure that lets us access information about the arguments passed to the UDF from the user such as the number of arguments provided and their values. The remaining arguments are a mix of `NULL` indicators and error message pointers. All of the arguments[4] and return requirements[5] for the API functions are documented in the MySQL manual.

Here's the implementation of our initialization function:

```
my_bool benford_init(UDF_INIT *initid, UDF_ARGS *args, char *message)
{
    /* verify incoming arguments */
    if (args->arg_count != 2) {
        strcpy(message, "function expects two arguments.");
```

---

[4] http://dev.mysql.com/doc/refman/5.6/en/udf-arguments.html

[5] http://dev.mysql.com/doc/refman/5.6/en/udf-return-values.html

```
        return 1;
    }
    /* coerce arguments - first arg to string will allow us to
       accept INT, DOUBLE, and REAL values (and also easier to
       extract most significant digit), the second arg must be
       INT to compare */
    args->arg_type[0] = STRING_RESULT;
    args->arg_type[1] = INT_RESULT;

    /* init shared data block */
    benford_data *data;
    if (!(data = (benford_data *)malloc(sizeof(benford_data)))) {
        strcpy(message, "Couldn't allocate memory");
        return 1;
    }
    data->seen = 0;
    data->rows = 0;
    initid->ptr = (char *)data;

    /* function will return 2 decimal places */
    initid->decimals = 2;

    return 0;
}
```

The init function verifies that the number of incoming arguments is correct (there should be two), coerces them to specific types to make our lives easier, allocates an instance of our benford_data structure, and sets the behavior of the function to return two decimal places. The benford_data struct is assigned to the pointer belonging to UDF_INIT so it can be passed between the various functions.

The clean-up function simply needs to free the shared struct so we don't have any memory leaks.

```
void benford_deinit(UDF_INIT *initid)
{
    free(initid->ptr);
}
```

At the beginning of each set of inputs, the clear function is invoked, which gives us an opportunity to initialize the tallies.

```
void benford_clear(UDF_INIT *initid, UDF_ARGS *args, char *is_null,
    char *error)
{
    benford_data *data = (benford_data *)initid->ptr;
    /* init values to 0 */
    data->seen = 0;
    data->rows = 0;
}
```

For each field in the set, MySQL calls the add function. This is where we look at the first digit in the number and decide whether it's the digit we're tracking or not. In either case, we'll increment the row counter so we can later calculate the percentage of the digit's appearance.

```
void benford_add(UDF_INIT *initid, UDF_ARGS *args, char *is_null,
    char *error)
{
    benford_data *data = (benford_data *)initid->ptr;
    data->rows++;

    if (args->args[0] && args->args[1]) {
        /* extract the leading digit — easy because it's a string */
        char *str = args->args[0];
        int i = str[0] - '0';

        int j = *((int *)args->args[1]);
        if (i && i == j) {
            data->seen++;
        }
    }
}
```

The main function calculates the Benford value as the percentage of times the digit appeared as the leading digit and returns it as a decimal. MySQL invokes this main function at the end of each group. If there's another group to process afterward—for example, if we're using GROUP BY in our SELECT statement—MySQL will call the clear function and begin working on the next set.

```
double benford(UDF_INIT *initid, UDF_ARGS *args, char* result,
    char *is_null, char *error)
{
    benford_data *data = (benford_data *)initid->ptr;
```

```
    if (data->rows) { /* no divide by zero! */
        return data->seen / (double)data->rows;
    }
    return 0.0;
}
```

The code needs to be compiled as a shared library and linked against the MySQL client libraries. Assuming your development toolchain is set up with gcc and you're at a Bash prompt, the compile command looks like this:

```
gcc -fPIC -shared -o udf_benford.so udf_benford.c \
    $(mysql_config --cflags) $(mysql_config --libs)
```

Compiling on Windows

Compiling on Windows is a bit more involved. Refer to the documentation[6] for guidance.

Work Through Compile Errors

The intricacies of coding and compiling C code are outside the scope of this book. If you run into trouble, read the error messages generated by your compiler and linker carefully and then consult the documentation to make sure you're doing things correctly. Sites like stackoverflow.com[7] can also be a good resource. Look through their archives to see if someone else has run into the same problem and found a solution.

The resulting module needs to be copied to MySQL's plugin directory which can be located by inspecting the value of the global system variable `plugin_dir`.

```
SHOW GLOBAL VARIABLES like 'plugin_dir';
+---------------+------------------------+
| Variable_name | Value                  |
+---------------+------------------------+
```

---

[6] http://dev.mysql.com/doc/refman/5.6/en/udf-compiling.html
[7] http://stackoverflow.com/

```
| plugin_dir    | /usr/lib/mysql/plugin/ |
+---------------+------------------------+
1 row in set (0.00 sec)
```

If MySQL is running on a system that uses AppArmor—a security layer that controls access to the file system beyond the standard permission system—it may be denied access to the files in the plugin directory. You can resolve the issue either by updating the AppArmor profile for MySQL, or by setting it to run in "complain" mode using aa-complain.

The last piece of the puzzle is to expose the functionality to the database by registering the UDF. For each function that's to be made available, a CREATE FUNCTION statement is executed that specifies the return type and the library file where the implementation can be found. If the UDF is an aggregate-value function, as our example is, then the statement should read CREATE AGGREGATE FUNCTION.

```
CREATE AGGREGATE FUNCTION benford RETURNS REAL
SONAME 'udf_benford.so';
```

Whenever you register a UDF, make sure the return type listed in the CREATE FUNCTION statement is what the function really returns. I've seen the same problem several times where someone cuts and pastes the statement from somewhere, changes the name of the function and library file, but forgets to touch the return type. In the best-case scenario, a mismatch will cause NULL values to be returned. In the worst, it could crash MySQL.

Once registered, we can use the function in our statements.

```
SELECT customer_id, benford(amount, 1) FROM payment
GROUP BY customer_id;

+-------------+--------------------+
| customer_id | benford(amount, 1) |
+-------------+--------------------+
|           1 |               0.03 |
|           2 |               0.04 |
|           3 |               0.12 |
:
|         598 |               0.00 |
```

```
|             599 |                  0.16 |
+-----------------+-----------------------+
599 rows in set (0.02 sec)
```

Conclusion

As you became acquainted with each routine presented in this chapter, hopefully you gained an appreciation of just how much power and flexibility they give us. You've learned about stored procedures, functions, triggers, and events. You've also seen how a UDF is written in C and accessed by MySQL. Whether to use them or not depends on what makes sense given what you're trying to accomplish. If you're writing an application that connects to MySQL and you want to code all logic in your app, that's fine. If you'll get better performance or gain flexibility by pushing that logic into the database, that's fine too.

If you find yourself writing stored routines in any serious capacity, you'll want to invest in proper development tools. For debugging, Debugger for MySQL[8] works well. It's a debugging IDE that supports breakpoints, watches, auto-completion, online help, and more. It's not free open-source software, but it runs on Windows and Linux under Wine and the developers offer a free, 14-day trial. For unit testing, frameworks are available that let you write tests in SQL like utMySQL[9] and STK/Unit[10]. The book *MySQL 5.1 Plugin Development*[11] by Sergei Golubchik and Andrew Hutchings may also serve you well if you want to write UDF functions and other MySQL plugins.

Take some time to play around with the concepts we've discussed here before moving on. In the next chapter, our time together will come to a close as we look at how to back up and restore MySQL databases and configure MySQL's replication service.

---

[8] http://mydebugger.com
[9] http://utmysql.sourceforge.net/
[10] http://stk.wikidot.com/stk-unit
[11] https://www.packtpub.com/big-data-and-business-intelligence/mysql-51-plugin-development

7

Backups and Replication

As our lives become more and more datacentric, the importance of having backups cannot be overstated. The effects of data loss can range from mildly irritating, such as losing your contacts list, to having a serious economic impact, such as a bank losing financial records. The more important your data is, and the more difficult it is to recreate, the more important it is to have backups.

I feel it's important to share with you a few ways to back up your MySQL databases before we say our goodbyes, so in this chapter we'll discuss making physical and logical backups. I'll also walk you through the steps to set up basic replication. Replication requires at least two MySQL installations—one to be the master and another to be the slave—so you'll need to install MySQL on another system if you plan on following along.

Logical Backups

A **logical backup** creates one or more files containing statements that can be used to reconstruct the database and its data. The files we downloaded in Chapter 3 from the MySQL website to set up the `sakila` database are one example of a logical backup. Such backups are portable, meaning they can be restored to pretty much any MySQL server with minimal fuss. But they can also take longer to create—and are slower to restore from—than other types of backups because the statements must be processed by MySQL.

Using `mysqldump`

We can use the command-line utility `mysqldump` that's included with MySQL to make logical backups. The program communicates with the server to retrieve our data and writes out the various statements capable of rebuilding the database. To make sure no changes are made during the process, we need to lock the tables with a "read lock" which makes the database read-only.

Follow these steps to make a logical backup of the `sakila` database using `mysqldump`:

1. In the command-line client, make sure `sakila` is the active database and issue a FLUSH TABLES statement so any pending operations are completed and the lock is established.

```
FLUSH TABLES WITH READ LOCK;
```

The lock will be in effect until we release it as long as this connection stays active.

2. Leave the client running in its current window and open a second terminal window or Command Prompt. In the second window, invoke `mysqldump`.

```
mysqldump -u root -p sakila > sakila-backup.sql
```

`mysqldump` outputs its statements to standard output, which is useful if you want to pipeline them as input to another command, but here I just redirect them to create the file `sakila-backup.sql`. The `-u` and `-p` options specify a user account, and prompt for a password to connect to MySQL (just like the command-line client), and `sakila` is obviously the database we're backing up.

3. Go back to the command-line client running in the first window and release the lock:

```
UNLOCK TABLES;
```

There are many options we can provide to `mysqldump` to get exactly what we want in our backup. The following is a brief list of some of the options you may find especially useful. For a complete list, you can either invoke the utility with `-?` or check out the documentation[1].

- `--add-drop-table` — include a `DROP TABLE` statement before any `CREATE TABLE` statements in the output. Without dropping a table first, the import process will fail on the `CREATE TABLE` statement when the backup is restored on a system that already has the tables defined.

- `--disable-keys` — add a statement that disables indexes and keys before the `INSERT` statements, and another statement afterwards to re-enable them. This can help speed up large imports, because MySQL can record its indexes all at once instead of after each `INSERT`.

- `--events` — export the definitions for any stored events associated with the database.

- `--hex-blob` — output binary values using hexadecimal notation. This can help protect against certain byte sequences being incorrectly interpreted, causing a restore to fail.

- `--tables` — back up only specific tables instead of all tables in the database. Any values after the option are treated as table names.

- `--triggers` — export the definitions for any triggers associated with the database.

- `--routines` — export the definitions for any stored procedures associated with the database.

- `--where` — a `WHERE` condition used to return only specific rows. For example, `--tables actor --where last_name LIKE 'B%'` will only export rows from the `actor` table for actors whose last name starts with B.

 Dump Files

You'll sometimes hear a backup file referred to as a "dump file," because the data has been dumped from the database into a file. I've let sophomoric humor get the

---

[1] http://dev.mysql.com/doc/refman/5.6/en/mysqldump.html

better of me a few times, telling my boss I'm going to "take a dump on the production server." Feel free to use the joke, but your mileage may vary.

Redirecting SELECT

Another way to make logical backups is to issue a SELECT statement, and redirect the data to a specific file using INTO OUTFILE. This approach backs up the table's data but not the table definition, so it's quite limited; but it's also said to be the fastest way to get data out of MySQL:

```
SELECT * FROM actor INTO OUTFILE '/tmp/actor.txt';
```

Exporting data in this manner is very restricted, for reasons of security. The output file can only be created on the host running MySQL, not the system you may be logged in from. The file also must not exist already. This prevents a malicious user from potentially overwriting sensitive system files.

The LOAD DATA statement imports data exported to a file in this manner:

```
LOAD DATA INFILE '/tmp/actor.txt' INTO TABLE actor;
```

Since INTO OUTFILE backs up the only the table's data—and with minimal structuring—importing the file could be problematic in some instances. The data is blindly loaded, so there is potential for key conflicts or duplicated rows if data already exists in the table. Check out the documentation for more information on INTO OUTFILE[2] and LOAD DATA[3].

Physical Backups

A **physical backup** is a raw copy of the files and directories managed by MySQL. Making a physical backup is generally faster than a logical backup, because it's really just a copy operation. But a drawback to physical backups is that they can't capture data that hasn't been persisted to disk—for example, tables managed by the MEMORY storage engine. If you recall from our discussion in Chapter 2, MEMORY keeps its data in RAM, so there are no files for us to copy. Also, physical backups are less

---

[2] http://dev.mysql.com/doc/refman/5.6/en/select-into.html
[3] http://dev.mysql.com/doc/refman/5.6/en/load-data.html

portable, and can only be restored to a similar system; a backup taken as an LVM snapshot on a Linux server can't be restored to a Windows system.

Before we can make a physical backup, we need to identify the directory that MySQL stores our data in. Inspecting the global system variable `datadir` will tell us the location:

```
SHOW VARIABLES LIKE 'datadir';
+---------------+----------------+
| Variable_name | Value          |
+---------------+----------------+
| datadir       | /var/lib/mysql/ |
+---------------+----------------+
1 row in set (0.00 sec)
```

Inside the data directory are separate directories for each of the databases that MySQL manages. In earlier times, when MyISAM was MySQL's principle storage engine, you could copy the database's directory and call it a day. MyISAM stores both: the table definitions and the data are stored together in the same directory. InnoDB is different, though. All data in InnoDB-managed tables, regardless of database, is stored together in `idbdata` files in the base data directory. Given that InnoDB is the default storage engine, I recommend backing up the entire data directory.

It's also important that MySQL doesn't attempt to modify any of the files during our backup procedure, which would result in a bad copy. We need to stop MySQL before starting the backup, and then restart it after we've finished.

Here's an example that makes a physical backup on Ubuntu:

```
sudo service mysql stop
sudo tar -cpzf /media/external/mysql-backup-$(date +%F).tgz \
  /var/lib/mysql
sudo service mysql start
```

The backup medium can be pretty much anything that suits your needs. If you're a developer, backing up a personal dev environment, you might copy them to an external hard drive. If you're working in an enterprise setting, the backup might be saved to a SAN, and later copied to high-capacity tape and shipped to an off-site storage facility.

To restore a physical backup, we need to stop MySQL, copy the files back into place, and then start MySQL:

```
sudo service mysql stop
sudo tar -C / --same-owner -xvzpf \
 /media/external/mysql-backup-YYYY-MM-DD.tgz
sudo service mysql start
```

There are many utilities for copying files and directories. Linux users have commands like `cp`, `tar`, and `cpio`, as well as LVM snapshots. Windows users have `xcopy` and `robocopy` and VSS (Volume Shadow Copy). And of course, both systems have a variety of dedicated backup applications as well.

Make Sure You Preserve Permissions

Whichever tool you use, make sure it can preserve the files' ownership and access permissions (this is what the `-p` flag does during compression, and what `-p` and `--same-owner` flags do during extraction in my examples above using `tar`). Otherwise, you'll need to reset the permissions after you restore the backup.

Replication

Replication is the ability for one or more **slave** servers to maintain a copy of another MySQL server's data. With replication enabled, when we add, update, and delete rows in the master server's database, details about the event are recorded to a special log file. The slaves then retrieve the logged details and repeat events to maintain their own local copy of the database, in near real time.

Useful Info

A **master** server doesn't wait for each slave to process an event; each slave is responsible for itself. That is, replication is an asynchronous process. Slave servers track their current position in the log, so we can bring a slave down for maintenance and it'll continue processing from the point it left off when we bring it back online.

Replication is useful in many different situations:

- Backups — we can stop replication on a slave server and we can make a physical backup of its data without affecting the availability of the master.

- Redundancy — if a full copy of the database is maintained on a slave, the master can be swapped out with a slave with little effort in failover or disaster-recovery scenarios.

- Scalability and performance — in heavy-load environments, write operations can be issued against the master, while read operations can be executed against read-only slaves, fanned out behind a load balancer.

There are three ways an event can be recorded in the log file: statement-based, row-based, and mixed-format logging. The default is **statement-based logging**, which records SQL statements that the slave will execute. **Row-based logging** writes details about every change the event effected. **Mixed-format logging** records SQL statements for most events, but switches to change details under certain circumstances. You can read about each approach, and the advantages and disadvantages of each, in the documentation[4].

 More on Replication

For a more detailed explanation of how replication works (beyond the 10,000 foot overview I've given here) check out this blog post by Aurimas Mikalauskas[5].

Setting up Replication

The following steps guide you through the process of configuring MySQL replication with one master and one slave. To complete the steps, you'll need two machines with MySQL installed—one which we'll designate as the master, and another as the slave.

1. Locate MySQL's configuration file on each system. The file is named **my.cnf** on Linux systems, and can be located using `find / -name my.cnf`. On Windows, it's named **my.ini**, and can be found using the Edge UI's Search charm.

2. Edit the master server's configuration file. If a configuration entry we want is commented out with a leading #, enable it by deleting the character. If the entry doesn't exist, add it under the `[mysqld]` section. The entries of interest are:

[4] http://dev.mysql.com/doc/refman/5.6/en/replication-formats.html
[5] http://www.percona.com/blog/2013/01/09/how-does-mysql-replication-really-work/

- server-id — identifies this server in the replication setup. It should be active (uncommented) and given a positive integer value unique between all of the servers in the group.

- log_bin — identifies the base name of the replication log file I mentioned earlier. This entry should be active.

- binlog_do_db — identifies which databases will be logged for replication. Multiple databases can be listed, separated by spaces. This entry should be active.

- skip_networking or bind-address — these entries configure whether MySQL accepts connections from the outside world or not. If skip_neworking is enabled, or bind-address is set to a value like 127.0.0.1, the master rejects the slave's connection attempts. We'll want these entries commented out.

Here are example values suitable for our master setup:

```
server-id = 1
log_bin = mysql-bin
binlog_do_db = sakila
# bind-address = 127.0.0.1
```

3. Save your changes to the master's configuration file and restart its MySQL instance.

4. Connect to the master with the command-line client, using the root user to create a new user account for the slave to use. We'll configure the slave to use this account to receive the replication details:

```
CREATE USER 'repluser'@'%' IDENTIFIED BY 'P@$$wOrd';
GRANT REPLICATION SLAVE ON *.* TO 'repluser'@'%';
FLUSH PRIVILEGES;
```

5. Take a backup of the master's database. We'll use the backup to populate the slave, to ensure it starts out in sync with the master.

   a. Lock sakila's tables:

```
FLUSH TABLES WITH READ LOCK;
```

b. Execute the dump command in a new terminal:

```
mysqldump -u root -p sakila > sakila-backup.sql
```

c. Return to the command-line client and release the lock:

```
UNLOCK TABLES;
```

6. Issue a SHOW MASTER STATUS statement to get information about the current state of the master. Remember the values the master reports back, because we'll need them to configure the slave:

```
SHOW MASTER STATUS;
+------------------+----------+--------------+------------------+
| File             | Position | Binlog_Do_DB | Binlog_Ignore_DB |
+------------------+----------+--------------+------------------+
| mysql-bin.000001 |      107 | sakila       |                  |
+------------------+----------+--------------+------------------+
1 row in set (0.00 sec)
```

7. Copy the master's backup file—made in step 5—over to the slave.

8. On the slave, create the sakila database and import the backup file:

```
mysql -u root -p -e 'CREATE DATABASE sakila'
mysql -u root -p < sakila-backup.sql
```

9. Open the slave server's configuration file and set the server-id value. Remember, the value must be unique among all servers in the replication group:

```
server-id = 2
```

10. Save the change to the configuration file and restart the slave MySQL instance.

11. With the command-line client, connect to the slave, and send the statement SHOW
    SLAVE STATUS\G to make sure its replication process is not running. If the value
    of Slave_IO_Running and Slave_SQL_Running aren't both "No," issue STOP
    SLAVE;.

> **Better Readability for Wide Output**
>
> The slave status presents a lot of fields that can be difficult to read because of
> line wrapping. Using \G to terminate the statement—instead of a semi-
> colon—causes the client to format the results vertically.

12. Send the following statement to the slave, to configure it to communicate with
    the master:

```
CHANGE MASTER TO
    MASTER_HOST = '192.168.1.100',
    MASTER_USER = 'repluser',
    MASTER_PASSWORD = 'P@$$w0rd',
    MASTER_LOG_FILE = 'mysql-bin.000001',
    MASTER_LOG_POS = 107;
```

The MASTER_HOST value is the address of your master server, MASTER_USER and
MASTER_PASSWORD are the credentials for the newly created replication account,
and MASTER_LOG_FILE and MASTER_LOG_POS indicate the current state of the
master's log file, as returned by the earlier SHOW MASTER STATUS statement.

13. Start the slave's replication process by sending START SLAVE;.

14. Verify that replication is running with a SHOW SLAVE STATUS statement. The
    values of Slave_IO_Running and Slave_SQL_Running should now both be "Yes."

To test that replication is working, make an update or insert a new row on the
master, and check the slave to see if the change propagated automatically.

Fixing Broken Replication

There are some things that aren't safe to do in a replicated environment, because
they can either break replication or result in inconsistencies between the master's
and slave's data. For example, inserting a row on a slave that would have otherwise

been replicated from the master is a no-no. Replication would attempt to insert a row that already exists, and thus cause an error. Using **nondeterministic functions** (functions that can return different values given the same input values) can also cause issues, especially when statement-based replication is used. For example, the NOW() function returns the current date and time. What was "now" on the master will not be "now" on the slave when the replicated statement is processed.

Whenever the slave encounters a problem, it will stop replication and wait for us to fix the issue. This behavior is ultimately a safety feature, because continuing on otherwise could potentially jeopardize the integrity of our data. Unfortunately, there is no notification when replication stops. Whether you use enterprise-grade tools like Nagios and Zabbix, or a homespun Bash script executed by cron, it's important to have some sort of monitoring in place.

When things go wrong, issue a SHOW SLAVE STATUS statement on the slave, and inspect the value of Last_SQL_Error to find out what the problem is. If things are irrecoverably broken, then rebuilding the slave's database may be your only option. But sometimes it's just one or two statements that get in the way—for example, a CREATE TABLE statement that failed to replicate because the table already existed on the slave. If that's the case, it's possible to skip the statement and let the replication process continue by issuing the following statements on the slave:

```
STOP SLAVE;
SET GLOBAL sql_slave_skip_counter = 1;
START SLAVE;
```

You can skip two statements by setting the global sql_slave_skip_counter variable to 2, three statements with 3, and so on. Be careful, though. If the failed statement is part of a transaction, the entire transaction will be skipped.

Plan Ahead

Now is the time to work out your backup procedures. People can be forgetful despite their best intentions, so an automated approach is preferable to one that relies on manual intervention. Each operating system comes with scheduling utilities: Linux distros have cron, and Windows has Task Scheduler. Even a dedicated backup utility worth its salt should have some scheduling capability.

Once you have your backups, decide how best to protect them. If you're working in a corporate environment, research the regulations, guidelines, and best practices for your particular industry. Typically, off-site storage of the backups is preferred. For personal backups, there are several free and commercial cloud backup providers.

You should also periodically test your backups. Make sure you're backing up the right files, and that you're able to restore them without issue. The middle of a crisis is never a good time to realize your backups are worthless.

The following table summarizes some of the pros and cons of the backup strategies discussed in this chapter:

	Logical	Physical	Replication
Pros	▦ Easy to implement ▦ More portable ▦ Able to selectively back up data ▦ Can back up MEMORY	▦ Easy to implement ▦ Faster to make ▦ Faster to restore ▦ Backups potentially use less space	▦ Doesn't affect master ▦ Near real time ▦ Log file can also be used for audit
Cons	▦ Slower to make ▦ Slower to restore ▦ Backups use more space because of SQL statements ▦ Must be scheduled	▦ Less portable ▦ Backups are not selective (all or nothing) ▦ Can only back up what's on disk ▦ Must be scheduled	▦ More involved setup ▦ Requires additional hardware ▦ Requires additional monitoring

Conclusion

In each chapter, I encouraged you to try out the concepts we covered, and undoubtedly you've started applying what you've learned in your day-to-day activities. Make sure that effort is safe by backing up your data, whether it's with logical backups, physical backups, or replication.

And with that, the time has come for us to part ways. Congratulations on reaching the end of the book! We've discussed a wide range of topics to bring you up to speed on as much MySQL as possible in the least amount of time. From installing MySQL and getting acquainted with its command-line client in Chapter 1 to working with multiple tables in Chapter 4, and familiarizing yourself with programming, both with and in MySQL, in Chapter 5 and Chapter 6, I trust you've learned a lot in these few pages.

Now go forth, dear friend, and spread your newfound wings.

CPSIA information can be obtained
at www.ICGtesting.com
Printed in the USA
BVOW11s1644250418
514393BV00003B/73/P